INDEXES AND INDEXING

INDEXES AND INDEXING

*Guide to the Indexing of Books, and Collections of Books
Periodicals, Music, Recordings, Films, and other
Material, with a Reference Section and
Suggestions for Further Reading*

by

ROBERT L. COLLISON

*Fellow of the Library Association
Vice-President, The Society of Indexers*

FOURTH REVISED EDITION

LONDON · ERNEST BENN LIMITED · 1972
NEW YORK · JOHN DE GRAFF INC

First published by Ernest Benn Limited 1953
25 New Street Square · Fleet Street · London · EC4A 3JA

and John de Graff Inc
34 Oak Avenue · Tuckahoe · NY 10707

Second Edition Revised and Enlarged 1959

Third Edition Revised and Enlarged 1969

Fourth Edition Revised and Enlarged 1972

© Robert Collison, 1972

Printed in Great Britain

ISBN 0 510–45722–3

To
D.M.C. and J.H.C.
who are inured to the sight
of many little slips being
shuffled and reshuffled
without any apparent result

Contents

7

Acknowledgements

SINCE THE FIRST EDITION of this book was published in 1953 there have been great and important developments in the complex field of modern indexing. For the information included in the new chapters, and for suggestions concerning the improvement of the original text, I owe much to Mr. G. Norman Knight, first Secretary of the Society of Indexers; Mr. F. L. Kent, formerly Librarian to UNESCO and now Librarian of the American Free University, Beirut; Miss Peggy Dowling of Shell Film Unit: Mr. D. J. Foskett, Librarian of the Institute of Education, University of London; Mr. C. W. Cleverdon, Librarian of the College of Aeronautics; Mr. John Askling, Lecturer on Indexing at the University of Columbia; Dr. A. G. Drachmann of Søborg; the late G. V. Carey, doyen of indexers; Professor Harold Borko of the University of California, Los Angeles; and Mr. E. T. Bryant, Borough Librarian of Widnes. I am also very much indebted to those who have taken part in the general, council and committee meetings of the Society of Indexers, for I have learnt much from their discussion of the problems we now face.

In the first edition of this book I wrote: Recognition of the care which any good publisher gives to the works he issues is all too rare. I cannot, however, let this opportunity pass of acknowledging my debt to Mr. Kenneth Day, of Messrs. Ernest Benn Limited, for the great interest he has taken in the production of this book at every stage. His many suggestions—and in particular the detailed attention he has given to the Reference Section—added substantially to any value which this volume may have for the reader. These remarks apply equally to the care and consideration which Mr. Day and his colleagues have given to this edition.

A little of the material in this book is reprinted or adapted from *Office Magazine* and from *The Indexer*, the bulletin of the Society of Indexers, and I am grateful to the Editors of those journals for permission to include it here.

R.L.C.

There is no greater literary sin than the omission of an Index, and, if I had my way, even novels would be provided with charts of this kind to their multifarious contents.

E. B. OSBORN: Literature and Life

Is there an indexer in the house?

The date, in these indexless books, is blown away again.

THOMAS CARLYLE:
Frederick the Great

A FRIEND OF MINE called Rarish had a curious experience in World War II. In due course he was drafted into a certain military unit and, as the only new recruit that day, had the unusual (and unsought) honour of being interviewed by the O.C. The O.C., a frightening man by any standards, stared at him ferociously for several seconds without speaking. Finally:

'You're a librarian?' he barked.

'Yes, sir,' answered Rarish nervously.

'Follow me!' commanded the O.C., brushing past him into the next room. There the scene was chaotic: row upon row of makeshift filing boxes filled with an untidy mass of cards were spread out on long trestle tables. The unit was a very large one and its personnel records were obviously in a very bad way. Too many cooks had had a finger in this pie.

'Get some order into this mess!' ordered the O.C. and strode out again. Rarish got down to it; with the aid of two ex-miners, a former chimney-sweep and a transferee from the Marines he got the whole mass of cards into one alphabetical sequence, with sufficient home-made signals to indicate the AWOLs, the sick, the non-existent and the other categories which needed special attention. In two days' time he reported himself ready for inspection. The O.C. marched in, accompanied by most of the available officers. Rarish saluted. The O.C. meticulously returned the salute.

'Give me the card relating to . . . 05234591 Brown, A. D.,' he ordered.

Rarish flicked through his cards, produced the entry within a matter of seconds. As the O.C. scrutinised the card there was a general murmer of amazement and appreciation from his satellites.

'Wait a moment, gentlemen,' muttered the O.C., 'may be just a flash in the pan.' He looked at Rarish:

'Good!' he said, 'now let me have 572835917 Cook, A. S.'

Rarish was quicker this time: the entry was in the O.C.'s hand almost as soon as he had finished speaking.

Virtue was never more quickly rewarded: Rarish was promoted, allowed to live out with his family, had a permanent pass to enter and leave camp at will. No-one ever told him to get a hair-cut. He was the camp's star turn: at every great inspection the brass-hats were brought to see Rarish's index, and it never failed to impress them with the efficiency of that noble unit.

Few people have such a spectacular opportunity of demonstrating the benefits of an efficient indexing system, but we have all had some such experience in our own office when an able has replaced a careless secretary, or after the reorganisation of a large stores department. The instinct to bring order into things is universal, but not everyone has the gift of accomplishing it.

Indexing is largely a matter of setting one's house in order. Nearly everyone does it in private life in some way or other, merely so that they can find things again when they need them. When a housewife makes a separate place for everything in the kitchen she is in fact creating a living index, for not only she, but all her household, will gradually get used to the system she has created and be able to discover things for themselves, even though it may involve knowing that sugar is always kept in a jar labelled SAGO. A man will get into the habit of always putting change in one pocket, keys in another, cigarette-case in a third—an elementary indexing habit which stands him in good stead when he checks up in his hurry to the station to see whether he has remembered his season-ticket. There is, in fact, no part of an orderly life which does not have some form of indexing as an essential part of its functioning, and many famous people would doubtless admit that they owe some measure of their success to the system they imposed on themselves early in their career.

None of the methods mentioned above is indexing as it is

generally understood today. The Victorian sewing-box with its hundred-odd compartments for different kinds of silks and threads, scissors and thimbles, depended on a visual approach and not on any written list of contents. But the index nevertheless did exist, not as a series of words but as a pattern in its user's mind. That pattern was so firmly embedded there that a glance would immediately grasp that something was missing or had been displaced—long before her memory told her what that thing was. This type of visual approach is a valuable asset which some people still develop in Kim's Game but which is not nearly enough exploited in present-day indexing: it is a faculty which is being allowed to atrophy along with all those other powers of touch and sight and smell which the gadgets of a machine age are encouraging us not to use. Some of the most famous detective stories are based on this lack of noticing power in modern times: the dog did not bark in the Sherlock Holmes' story of *Silver Blaze*; the postman did not call in Raymond Chandler's *Farewell, My Lovely*, and the significance of the non-occurrence of an ordinary event was missed by the onlookers because the ability to react to a break in an everyday sequence had become weakened.

Thus, if all man's original faculties were left intact there would be no reason to index anything at all by modern methods. For instance, in the old days great folk epics were communicated by word of mouth and each singer of the exploits of Hereward the Wake and King Arthur learnt his song by rote from the ancient minstrels of the time. Such men had no need of an index to *Beowulf* such as we are obliged to use today, for they knew every word of the saga and, if asked where such and such a phrase occurred, could usually take up the recital at that point after a moment's thought. Such great memories still survive, but mostly among members of African tribes who have not yet succumbed to the temptations of print and textbook learning. Nor is the loss of this type of folk memory altogether a bad thing, for though the Arab child may learn part of the Koran by heart in his schooldays, he may have to neglect many other more practical subjects in order to do so; and since we are now having to grapple with a thousand facets of a complex industrial civilisation, it is just as well that we should embrace such modern substitutes as logarithms, and indexes and formulae, so that we can leave our memories free to cope with problems other than the art of learning by rote the exact position, or wording, of single passages in a few books.

Indexing has thus come to stay and, from the point of view of the advance of modern civilisation, it is a great pity that this fact was not recognised sooner. For example, in the eighteenth century the British government was still printing the Statutes of the realm without any form of index beyond a wordy list of contents. Even the first great dictionaries of French, Spanish and Italian were arranged by the roots of words instead of the modern alphabetical order with which we are familiar today. In the *Gentleman's Magazine* it was the custom until well into the nineteenth century to list in the index all the people named Smith who died in a single year without any indication of their initials or full Christian names. Such practices as these, which were common enough at the time to escape criticism, cause needless waste of time today, but not half as much difficulty as the *lack* of indexing in the old indexes: it is possible to look in vain in the old indexes of the mid-nineteenth-century files of the *Illustrated London News* for items which you know you have seen somewhere in those vast and unwieldy volumes. Much of this was of course due to what might well be called 'critical indexing' since it was based on the assumption that 'no-one will ever want a reference to *that*.' Much more was owing to the fact that people just did not know how to index properly, their ideas of what was suitable for index entries being limited to simple things like proper names and straightforward events.

So it happens that when anyone comes to write the history of his family, the story of an old-established commercial or industrial undertaking, or the chronicle of his town, he will assuredly run into unexpected and bewildering difficulties. For the immediate past half-century the events may perhaps be clear enough, but the happenings of the preceding twenty years may take twice as long to discover because the system of indexing of that time may have been different or less efficient. In the old chronicles and histories it was the custom of the clerk or historian to write in the wide margins brief descriptive phrases indicating the main points dealt with in the long paragraphs. Consistency in emphasis was only maintained as long as the same man was doing the work, but as soon as a new scribe took over his ideas of what might be worth emphasis would almost certainly differ from those of his predecessor. In the same way modern indexes vary very much in quality and system, and only those who have made a long study of the average modern index of any size can possibly get out of it all that it can offer to its users. It would be true to say that there arc very few indexes in existence which would not benefit from being done again, starting with the indexes to *The Times* for the first hundred years of its publication, and proceeding through most books of law and medicine, as well as the larger histories and encyclopaedias.

While some of the chapters which follow in this book try to show how such a task could be tackled, the majority of them cover subjects of more immediate interest in contemporary life and set out to indicate how indexing can be used to make life easier and more efficient, to eliminate time- and money-wasting and to avoid mistakes and irritation. Indexing is not a panacea for all modern evils but it can certainly be a palliative for some of the more common of them.

A little
history

*An index is a necessary implement . . .
without this, a large author is but a
labyrinth without a clue to direct the
readers within.*

THOMAS FULLER

THE INSTINCT TO MAKE a guide to information has always been very strong in mankind. It is even recorded that a temple library of the Middle East in the pre-Christian era had its catalogue incised in stone on a tablet set in one of the walls of the chamber. With the coming of books as we know them, inventories or catalogues of books were common in most monasteries, and in the fourteenth century at least two attempts were made to compile complete lists (with the location of each copy carefully marked) of the books in the various religious centres in England, for the benefit of itinerant monks, and these attempts were made on remarkably modern lines.

Guides to individual books commenced early too: chapter headings are as old as books themselves, and contents lists were soon introduced. Another method was to insert paragraph headings in the margins—or as indents in the paragraphs themselves—a popular system which has survived until today in such books as Saintsbury's *Short History of English Literature* and Bury's *History of Greece*. Another method which has become permanent is the system of printing a descriptive headline at the top of each page; in some books this headline changes with each page, but more frequently it just repeats the book or chapter title.

It was soon realised, however, that such methods were at best only rough-and-ready, and were not sufficient for the needs of serious readers. But indexing, in the sense in which it is understood today, is an advanced art, and its principles were not very easily grasped at first. The word index thus came to include a number of systems of guiding which would not be described as indexes now. Sometimes it denoted a list of contents, at other times a summary, and at other times a number of notes, but very rarely did it represent the scientific arrangement of today. It must, however, be admitted that some of the so-called indexes published by contemporary periodicals are no more worthy of the name.

The necessity for indexes came to the fore in men's minds once the English Bible was made available to ordinary people. However much a man might read and study The Book he could not hope to remember every time the context of the words which he wished to refer to or quote. The urge is exemplified in the life of the gifted but eccentric Alexander Cruden who devoted several years to the compilation of the first complete Concordance to the Bible.[1] This was indeed indexing on a grand scale, and the value of his efforts is shown in the fact that his Concordance is still in daily use, although it is now well over two centuries old (1737).

Cruden's Concordance was by no means the first good index, but there is no doubt that his example provided a useful stimulant to the achievement of high standards by other contemporary indexers. In fact, the eighteenth century was the first great age of the index: Cruden indexed only the Bible—Johnson indexed the English language itself. Dr. Johnson, moreover, displayed a degree of business ability which cannot always be claimed by great literary men. He employed six scribes, his method being to mark the passages he wished to be transcribed, together with the index words under which they were to appear. It seems, however, as though the indexer of the day was usually a man of inferior status. Goldsmith, in his mock letters from a Chinaman entitled the *Citizen of the World*, speaks contemptuously of an author with exaggerated claims to fame: 'he writes indexes to perfection'.

Nevertheless, many books of the period went without indexes, and others failed to benefit greatly from the standards of clarity and consistency set by Johnson and Cruden: a glance, for instance, at the volumes of the *Statutes at large* of this period will show that the contemporary lawyer must have had to rely

[1] Henry B. Wheatley points out that John Marbeck made a Concordance to the Bible in 1550.

B

largely on his memory and on any private indexing he was able to do for himself.

In the next century indexing improved both in execution and in the esteem of the public. Isaac Disraeli himself declared that he venerated the inventor of indexes and knew not whether to do him or Hippocrates more honour. Lord Campbell considered an index to be essential to every book, and proposed to bring a Bill into Parliament to 'deprive an author who publishes a book without an index of the privileges of copyright, and, moreover, to subject him for his offences to a pecuniary penalty'. But his idea never became law and books have suffered much thereby. On the other hand, the work of making indexes to their books is distasteful to most authors, and Lord Campbell's proposal would probably have done more to increase the numbers of professional indexers than the number of author-indexers.

The publication of periodicals was greatly stimulated and increased by the rapid development of printing machinery in the nineteenth century. By the 'forties both *Punch* and the *Illustrated London News* had come into existence. Their indexes were, however, extremely poor, as any modern research worker soon discovers once he attempts to search their files. In fact, the initiative for making good indexes to periodicals seems to have passed to the United States where the next important developments took place.

While in London Palmer's small quarterly indexes to *The Times* were probably as detailed as any indexing in Britain at that time, across the Atlantic W. F. Poole was preparing the way for his great indexes to the periodicals of the nineteenth century. These were a new advance, and a considerable one: instead of an index to one periodical for one year, Poole introduced the idea of one index to many periodicals covering a considerable number of years.

But both Poole's and Palmer's indexes, together with those of the majority of books, were to a certain extent unsatisfactory. The reader might be fortunate enough to find the passage for which he was looking. On the other hand, he might not. It all depended on his skill in hitting upon the right heading in the index. The influence of Germany had made itself felt in the system which was widespread at that time: this was, the selection of the *Schlagwort* or catchword for entering an item. Thus, two articles, respectively entitled 'A short review of the drama of the nineteenth century' and a 'Brief conspectus of the theatre in the nineteenth century' would, under Poole's system have been entered:

> Drama of the nineteenth century, Short review of.
> Theatre of the nineteenth century, Brief conspectus of.

This is an improvement on the system of indexing these articles under 'A' or 'Short' or 'Brief', but it is still only a distant approach to the scientific methods of today, which would ensure that the reader discovered these items whether he remembered or not the actual terms used in their titles. An improvement was not long in coming: the great H. W. Wilson started his *Readers' Guide to Periodical Literature* in 1901. Nothing like this had ever been seen before. Each article in a periodical was indexed under its author and under its specific subject. There were numerous cross-references to link up each subject with related subjects and with aspects of itself, and a very high standard of consistency and accuracy was maintained from the first. This was but the beginning of a long series of brilliant indexes, both general and specialised, issued by the same firm, which set the pace and the pattern for continuative indexing in the twentieth century. Today, the house of H. W. Wilson of New York is known throughout the world for its valuable contribution to present-day research.

Meanwhile book-indexing was improving. During the nineteenth century many long sets of books were published and skill in indexing increased with the experience thus gained. One of the outstanding examples was the index to the *Encyclopaedia Britannica*, which was an astonishing achievement of detail and conciseness, as well as a masterpiece of clarity and layout. In the accounts books of the great commercial houses of the period it is also noticeable that a manuscript index of names of traders, etc., was kept in considerable detail.

The twentieth century can truly be called the great age of indexing. It is very much the outcome of the need to provide a key to the growing mass of information which is accumulating so rapidly that no-one can grasp its immensity. No person who is engaged in the work of extracting information from printed sources—be he librarian, information officer, journalist, secretary, scientist, or research worker, etc.—can fail to be aware of the frustration constantly presented by knowing that the information exists, without knowing *where* it exists. But heroic efforts have been made to overcome these difficulties. Private societies have set themselves to index old books, parish registers, archives, and all kinds of material. Old indexes have been done over again, and some of the indexers have gone back in history in an endeavour to get the most out of what is still extant. Others have tried to keep abreast of the mass of material pouring from the Press each day.

Indexing has outstripped the idea of previous ages: from indexes to individual works, we have progressed through indexes to several volumes, to co-operative indexes on an international scale. There are at present great international indexes to books and periodicals on such subjects as international affairs, forestry, education, and all kinds of other subjects. Even so, there are still greater possibilities and it will be interesting to watch the developments of the next few decades in this field.

In spite of all this progress, the average book index lags sadly behind as though all these developments had never taken place. Quite a large number of British books, and a smaller number of American books, are still published without indexes. What is nearly as bad is that most books appear with totally inadequate indexes, and the reasons are first, that very few people know how to index properly, and secondly, that most publishers do not encourage the provision of really adequate indexes. It has been said by more than one publisher that, in the case of small books at least, indexes are unnecessary, the contents page being sufficient. But in most cases publishers admit the need for an index and then allot too little space for it. It is quite usual to find a book of two hundred and fifty pages with an index of four pages only. Such little space is insufficient for all but the barest finding list. One of the most usual omissions is that of the titles and authors of the books mentioned in the text. Another common fault is the omission of references to ideas and concepts, references being made to people, places and chapter headings only.

Even where the index approaches adequate proportions there

are often numerous defects. It is an everyday occurrence to find a whole string of page references to a subject, without any differentiation between those which merely mention the subject and those which treat it in detail, and without any indication of the aspects discussed. Quite often certain parts of a book are not indexed at all: illustrations are usually omitted, and few indexes cover prefaces, forewords, introductions, footnotes, bibliographies—or even page-headings. There are arguments that can be brought forward to justify this practice, but none which will satisfy the angry reader who cannot find some item he remembers hc has sccn somewhere in the book.

In these days of rapid advances and developments every method that can be adopted to assist the research worker and the ordinary reader is not only justified, it is imperative. Life is too short to waste time searching for information which may or may not exist in the book that is being examined. Every serious reader knows that it is possible to search time and time again for a lost item. This is easily remedied, and the work involved should not be shirked by authors or their publishers.

Amateur indexing still continues: stories are still current of poets who eke out an uncertain livelihood by indexing books on subjects of which they know little or nothing, and of authors who contrive indexes to their own works with very little attention to accuracy or comprehensiveness. Without wishing to deprivc thc poet of his means of living, or the author of responsibility for his own work, the reading public has nevertheless a right to better treatment. The reading public is of course partly to blame—it accepts without much audible complaint the wretched substitutes for indexes so often offered it. Few readers know what a really good index could be, or what it could do for them. When a really adequate index is for once provided it is taken for granted without any general realisation or appreciation of the amount of time and skill that have gone to its making.

This small book is devoted to the task of explaining the basic rules on which all good indexing must rest, and to showing how they may be applied in practice to the many different problems which confront the indexer. Because so many people find it necessary to maintain their own private indexes of such material as correspondence, gramophone records, trade literature, pamphlets, and other un-bookish items, space has been found to indicate sound ways of setting about such tasks. The main principle is consistency, and if the system adopted can—by judicious expansion, and without undue alteration—cope with twenty thousand almost as easily as with two hundred items, the indexer may have good cause to be pleased with his efforts.

Part one

The
indexing
of books

General principles

THE ONE PURPOSE in making an index to any book is to make all the information in that volume fully available to any reader without delay. This is a comparatively simple matter as far as it concerns references to names of places and of people—though, as will be seen later, even these can present difficulties—but some skill and experience are required wherever it is desired to make references to ideas and define and indicate the different aspects of a subject. Indexing, in fact, is no mechanical process: if it is to be of use, it requires thought and consideration in every phase of its construction.

The first step in the process of indexing must be to put oneself in the position of the reader as far as possible, bearing in mind too that one reader may differ from another in his knowledge of the subject and in his approach to the book. This at once raises the question whether the author is the best person to index his book. On the one hand, the author knows more than anyone else about his book, but on the other, he may find it difficult, if not impossible in some cases, to view it from the point of view of the reader who does not know as much as he does about the subject. A professional indexer has the advantage of knowing the mechanics of his work very well, and of seeing things from a broader standpoint, but on the other hand, he may not always be able to interpret the author's intention nearly as well as the author would wish.

It is not possible to lay down the law on this point. Each case must be considered individually. The most which can be said is that if the author indexes his own book, his index will benefit by being submitted to knowledgeable readers for their suggestions and criticisms. If, however, the book is indexed by another person, the closest collaboration between author and indexer is necessary, if the index is to achieve a good standard.

In either case, the book should first be read through two or three times as a whole. This is a very useful preliminary, especially if passages are underlined and notes made[1] as the book is read, for the reader—whether author or professional indexer—can size up the approximate amount of attention paid to various subjects, the desirability of various references and headings, and the necessity for including or omitting references to minor items. If this preliminary reading is not done, the indexer will undoubtedly regret it before he has completed many references.

The way is now clear to commence the indexing. References are best entered on slips, and care should be taken in selecting a suitable size and consistency of paper. All the slips should be of the same size, to facilitate sorting, and they should be made of fairly stiff paper or card since this enables them to be separated and filed more easily, and prevents any slips being overlooked. Experience has shown that a useful size of slip is one about 7 in. by 2 in., although some indexers prefer a semi-stiff card of about 5 in. by 3 in.

If the book is still in manuscript form the index can be made in one of the following ways. If each paragraph has been numbered and the numbers are to be printed, it is possible to complete the index before going to press by making the references to the paragraph numbers instead of to the pages. If no paragraph numbers are to be printed, the indexer can number each paragraph in pencil for the purpose of his index, and enter these paragraph numbers in pencil on his slips. When the page proofs arrive, the indexer sorts his slips into order of paragraph numbers, and can then rapidly substitute page for paragraph numbers. The slips are then re-sorted alphabetically, ready for typing. In this way, the index is ready by the time the page proofs are returned for correction, and the progress of the book through the press is not impeded by any delay over the index.

Most books however are indexed from the page proofs. This does not preclude the possibility of giving paragraph instead

[1] On slips, or in the margins of the proofs of the book itself.

of page-number references. Indeed, in the case of books with large pages or much complicated information, which cannot readily be grasped by a general glance at the page, paragraph references are desirable. Very large books, such as the *Encyclopaedia Britannica*, go further and divide up the individual page into areas, giving references by page and position on the page, so that, for instance, 1455b will indicate the lower left-hand section of page 1455. Classical and modern verse texts, where exact reference is necessary owing to the recurrence of similar words and phrases, are often numbered line by line, which enables the bulk of the indexing to be carried out in the manuscript stage.

Having decided what kind of slips to use, and whether references are to be made to paragraph or page numbers, the indexer then proceeds to draft his references. It is a good rule to confine each slip to one subject-reference, and to keep all slips in one alphabetical order right from the beginning. To facilitate this, it is useful to have a small tray with three sides, just large enough to hold about one thousand slips. The sides should be about one-eighth of an inch lower than the slips, so that they can easily be turned over and referred to, and so that they can be inserted and withdrawn without difficulty. If there are likely to be many slips, stiff cards about a quarter of an inch taller should be inserted to act as guides and to break up the slips into the letters of the alphabet. In the case of 5 in. by 3 in. cards, suitably printed guide cards of this description can be purchased from most stationers, and there are also larger sets of guide cards which can break up the sequence into any number of parts.

If the book is already in page proof, the indexer is in a position to find out from the publisher how much space has been allotted to the index, and this he should do since otherwise his index may prove to be too detailed, and the consequent revision to fit the available space may not only be wearisome but also produce faults. From the number of pages available it is possible to calculate the exact number of references which can be made. For instance, an eight page demy-octavo index set in 8-Point will allow 62 lines to the page, and thus not more than 992 references can be made in a *double-column* index of this size. This number must however be scaled down slightly, for allowance must be made for the title 'Index', for any explanation of method of use, and for any headings and spaces between each letter of the alphabet. These can easily be calculated by comparison with printed indexes in other books, but as a rough guide an allowance of forty-six to fifty references for space occupied in this way should be borne in mind in constructing any index, whatever its size.

It must also be kept in mind that in any length of line—and most index lines are very short—some references will overlap into the next line, and that the addition of aspects, etc., to the original subject reference may involve the use of two or more lines. For example, the average half-column line used for indexes in crown and demy-octavo books will not allow more than about 38 letters and spaces in a single line of average 8-point type, so that the heading 'Union of the Christian Churches and Sects' would have to be broken in this fashion:

> Union of the Christian Churches and
> Sects, 24, 26, 29–31

Since the indexer's ideas on how much can be squeezed into an index may not conform with what is typographically possible, it is wise to make a further allowance of ten or more references for difficulties of this kind. In all, therefore, the indexer should make a total allowance of a minimum of sixty references for title, headings, spaces, and unforeseen overlapping, so that in the example given above he would limit himself to about 930 references, each line counting as one reference.[1] In a later chapter some hints will be given on some economies that can be effected which will allow more references to be made without increasing the size of the index.

While limiting each slip to one subject, it is however possible to include aspects of the subject on the same slip, if these are not too many. Perhaps a word on the question of aspects at this point would not be amiss.

Whereas a subject is a distinct idea, such as fishing, coalmines, painting, etc., an aspect is a feature of a subject. Thus in the term ARMY DISCIPLINE, Discipline is an aspect of the word Army, and on the index slip would be entered:

---

[1] In Part III, a table of estimated numbers of entries for different sizes of pages is given—see p. 187.

> Army
> > discipline

the subject being written near the top left-hand corner of the slip or card, and the aspect being indented three spaces (or more, if desired) below. Assuming that the Army figures largely in the book to be indexed, and that discipline, pay, leave, and promotion are discussed on pages 15, 35, 28 and 127 respectively, the entries on the slip would be entered:

> Army
> > discipline, 15
> > leave, 28
> > pay, 35
> > promotion, 127

and the aspects are arranged either then or later in alphabetical order. This assumes that the Army is only one of several different subjects discussed in the book. Were the book, on the other hand, wholly devoted to the subject of the Army, each of these aspects would probably be discussed in much greater detail, and would then rank as main subjects, each with its own slip:

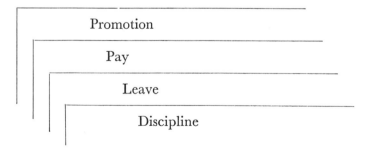

> Promotion
> > Pay
> > > Leave
> > > > Discipline

and would perhaps have other aspects of their own, as for instance:

> Discipline, 37–68
> eighteenth-century, 21
> nineteenth-century, 28–9

in which the first reference—pages 37 to 68—would probably represent a whole chapter devoted to the subject of Discipline, and the other references to incidental mentions in a preliminary historical account.

In the choice of subject-headings it is especially necessary to consider the kind of people likely to use the book. If, for instance, the book is directed towards scientific readers it is best to use scientific rather than popular headings, and to use such terms as AGRICULTURE rather than FARMING, ORNITHO-LOGY rather than BIRDS. The reverse is true of popular books, but where there is any doubt, or where both types of reader are likely to make use of the book, it is safer to choose the popular forms of headings. Consistency in this, as in all other things connected with indexing, is essential if the index is to be used easily. From the form of heading not used, it is advisable to make a reference:

> Agriculture *see* Farming
>
> Ornithology *see* Birds

and the indexer should constantly bear in mind the possibility of the existence of synonyms or near synonyms from which such references should be made. It must be remembered that some potential users of the book will perhaps first glance at the index to see if the subjects covered include any of interest to them, and that the insertion of synonymous headings will be of material assistance.

By keeping the slips in alphabetical order from the beginning, much duplicate writing of headings is avoided and control is maintained over the eventual size of the index throughout the process. Thus, in a book on big-game hunting, if Lions are mentioned on pages 13, 72, and 119 to 228, a slip is made for the first reference, and when the subsequent mentions are reached the slip is withdrawn from its alphabetical sequence and the additional references entered on it:

Lions, 13, 72, 119–228

Thus, while the making of the index will be slow at the beginning, owing to the necessity for writing many slips, it will gradually become more speedy as less and less headings have to be written, and the work becomes mainly one of adding aspects and page references to the existing slips. To this end, it is wise to add references from synonymous headings as soon as they come to mind, to avoid waste of effort in making duplicate entries under different headings.

It will be found, generally speaking, that while the indexer will usually carry in his head quite easily the headings he has used during the first twenty to thirty pages, his memory will not always record them all during the subsequent indexing, especially if this takes place over a lengthy period. The making of references from synonymous headings will therefore assist him in turning to the main headings which he has previously decided to use, and this is the more desirable, since any revision or rewriting involves the ever-present risk of error in recopying page-references.

Clear writing is essential, whatever the form in which the manuscript index finally reaches the printer. Nothing is more vexatious to the reader than to find a reference for which no justification exists on the page mentioned. Another error which occurs occasionally, is the cross-reference which refers back to itself, in a vicious circle, such as:

Wireless *see* Radio

Radio *see* Wireless

Stephen Leacock has ruthlessly summarised this danger in his brilliant essay on 'The Perfect Index':

What is the real title or name of a thing or person that has three or four? Must you put everything three or four times over in the Index, under three or four names? No, just once, so it is commonly understood; and then for the other joint names, we put what is called a cross-reference, meaning, see this, or see that. It sounds good in theory, but in practice it leads to such results as '*Talleyrand, see Perigord . . .*' and when you hunt this up, you find—*Perigord, Bishop of,* see *Talleyrand.* The same effect can be done flat out, with just two words, as *Lincoln,* see *Abraham . . . Abraham,* see *Lincoln.* But even that is not so bad because at least it's a closed circle. It comes to a full stop. But compare the effect, familiar to all research students, when the circle is not closed. Thus, instead of just seeing Lincoln, the unclosed circle runs like this, each item being hunted alphabetically, one after the other—*Abraham,* see *Lincoln . . . Lincoln,* see *Civil War . . . Civil War,* see *United States . . . United States,* see *America . . . America,* see *American History . . . American History,* see also *Christopher Columbus, New England, Pocahontas, George Washington . . .* the thing will finally come to rest somehow with the dial pointing at: See *Abraham Lincoln.*

This kind of peril can only be avoided by careful checking when the index has been completed, but it can be prevented to a great extent during the process of making an index by ensuring that every reference made does—at that time, at least—lead to a valid mention.

Indexing at speed

ONE OF THE DIFFICULTIES which puts off most people almost
as soon as they start making an index is the boredom of the
process. Indexing is abandoned as often as any other hobby.
There are however many short cuts to indexing which can not
only relieve the tedium but also speed up the process without
any loss in efficiency: they do in fact make the index more
efficient and economical. The most effective short cut is of
course the elimination of all unnecessary entries and the concentration on those which will be definitely useful. This is
easier to do in an index which will be used by oneself, or by a
limited group of people who are constantly consulting the index
in conjunction with each other, than in a purely general index
designed for public use. Thus a large factory may have an
index or inventory of its stores which will omit many entries—
since all members of the staff will know the correct designation
of the items they handle—and may abbreviate many more than
would be so treated in an index used by all and sundry.

Even in general indexes much waste still occurs, mainly
because of the survival of traditional methods which have out-
lived their day. To test this statement, examine one or two
pages of any sizeable index with which you may be acquainted
and make a note of the number of headings under which you
yourself would not think of seeking that information. To do so
it will be necessary to compare the index entries with the relevant passages in the text, and to judge how successfully those
entries describe the subject matter. From such a list it will be
necessary to remove any item under which you feel other

people might perhaps look—even so, you may often be left with a fair number of points. Multiply these by the proportionate number of pages of the index and you may find that the index could well have been a page or half-a-page shorter. This is no mere question of just saving space: the larger the index the longer the time needed to find any single entry—a point which can be proved by comparing the time taken to find ten pre-determined entries in a ten-page and a twenty-page index respectively.

To take an actual example of the over-elaboration of index-ing let us consider Thomas Carlyle's *The French Revolution: a History* in Thomas Nelson's elegant india-paper edition of 1902. In this 880-page volume the generally excellent index occupies only twenty-six pages, not an unreasonable size for such a large book. Yet take such entries as these:

> Applauder, hired, 469, 478
> Blood, baths of, 11
> Gifts, patriotic, 556
> Ideals, realized, 8
> Man, Rights and mights of, 201, 209, 473
> Past, the, and Fear, 621
> Present, the, and Fear, 621
> Verbs, Irregular, National Assembly at, 198
> Youth, Gilt, 815, 828

Are these entries really necessary in any but a concordance of Carlyle's writings?—which this index certainly does not set out to be. 'Applauder, hired' refers to Carlyle's descriptions of 'Hand-clappers or *clacquers*' under neither of which terms is there any index entry. 'Blood, baths of' indexes the following sen-tence: 'That Law authorizing a Seigneur, as he returned from hunting, to kill not more than two Serfs, and refresh his feet in their warm blood and bowels, has fallen into desuetude—and even into incredibility', but there are no entries in the index for Hunting or for Serfs and those for Seigneurs and Law have no references to this passage. The entry for 'Gifts, patriotic' seems merely to have been inspired from the fact that these words stand out on page 556 by reason of their initial capitals, and the same reason would appear to apply in the case of the entry for 'Ideals realized'. The entries relating to the Past and Fear and the Present and Fear are puzzling since there is no reference from Fear, and the mystifying words Irregular Verbs at the National Assembly turn out to be a more than thorough indexing of one of Carlyle's own verbal explosions. 'Youth, Gilt' refers to the passage 'Fréron, in his fondness, names them *Jeunesse Dorée*, Golden or Gilt Youth' (page 815) and 'Money-changer Sections and Gilt Youth sweep them forth, with steel besom, far into the depths of Saint-Antoine' (page 828), but there is no consistency here for there are no entries or references under *Jeunesse Dorée*, Golden, Gilt, or Money-changer sections.

Nor are these criticisms derogatory to such a good index: they are purely examples of what can happen when working too close to the material. In such circumstances, the unexpected and the unusual assume an importance out of all proportion to their real merits—and, in Carlyle's case his very style adds all its persuasive force. The only remedy is the revision of the index on completion and, preferably, its testing by other people. Such inspection would reveal that, while there is an entry 'Man, Rights and Mights of', there is no entry under 'Rights of Man'.

But apart from pruning and revising indexes, and from effecting economies by utilising to the full the variations offered by modern type-setting, there are still other opportunities open to the progressive indexer who is willing to take a little trouble with his preliminary work. One of the great problems inherent in any large-scale indexing is the vast number of index slips which must be handled once the process of indexing is really under way, and these present very real physical difficulties. A set of five hundred slips, for instance, is not unmanageable: it can be balanced on a tray or in a strong cardboard box on the arm of an easy-chair, and the indexing can proceed under the most favourable conditions—by one's own fireside. Once the index gets beyond a thousand entries a table is needed and all the paraphernalia and conditions of office work. The job has become a task, and even the work of extracting and sorting away entries becomes slower and more tedious and tends to delay progress, for it is necessary to keep the references sorted away as soon as they are made if ambiguities are to be avoided. Thus, as the index grows the work slows up and the boredom increases—conditions which are inimical to the making of good indexes.

Some of this can be avoided by planning the whole process

from the start and by a rigid and consistent control of entry-making. The system to be described is one which can only be used where there is a single indexer, for it depends entirely on the consistency which can only obtain where but one mind is involved in the work of choosing the most appropriate subject-headings. Apart from this, any indexer can immediately put the scheme into operation with considerable savings in time, space and stationery.

In a nutshell, this particular system eliminates the use of separate index slips for most references, added entries and alternative headings. It reduces the number of index slips to be handled by at least fifty per cent, and helps to strengthen the index by reminding the indexer, throughout the work he is doing, of what references and added entries have been made to date, so that the questions which constantly arise in his mind during conventional indexing concerning the necessity for additional references, etc., are straightway answered without his having to refer to several different places in his files of index slips. The control thus exerted makes for more confident and efficient indexing, relieves the indexer of some of the strain caused by conventional indexing, cuts down the number of possibilities of wrong page-references, and adds to the indexer's chances of envisaging his work as a whole during the entire process of indexing either books or periodicals.

Suppose, for example that reference is made in a book on architecture to a Rebate or Door-check which Sir Alfred Clapham, in his *Romanesque Architecture in England* (London: Longmans, Green (for the British Council), 1950, page 44) defines as: 'The set-back of the jamb of a doorway against which the door must come to rest.' Under this new indexing system the indexer, on first coming across a reference to a Rebate makes an entry under this word, and notes possible references at the foot of his index slip:

Rebate, 21	
Door-check	Door (s/a)
Check, Door-	Jamb (s/a)
Set-back (Door)	

In doing so he commits himself to nothing, beyond the fact that he has noted that he must eventually decide what references and added entries he must make with regard to the term Door-check. He has noted all the possible direct references and has included two general references from which he must consider making 'see also'—(*s/a*)—references, if he ultimately decides they may be needed. This is a very useful position in which to be, for the indexer may be inclined to change his mind as he proceeds through the book and discovers that the term Door-check is used more often than Rebate, so that he may eventually finish with a revised entry slip:

Door-Check, 21, 36, 92, 96

refs. Check, Door-   *s/a* Door
        Rebate   Jamb
        Set-back (Door)

---

or, more probably, this entry will prove to be the original slip with the heading and the first reference transposed or crossed out and rewritten. The indexer's decision to change the main heading has been made the easier by the fact that he has been able to change no less than six entries by an alteration on a single slip, without any of the possibilities of error which the recopying of page-references, etc., on six separate slips might have entailed.

The subsequent control of these slips for the final typing of the index is dependent on a certain amount of preliminary editing and on a consistent routine when transferring the entries to the typescript. When editing the slips for typing, each slip with more than one heading on it is marked so that whatever the order in which the headings appear on the slip their alphabetical order is immediately apparent. The slip shown above would now appear as indicated overleaf.

When all the slips have been treated in this fashion they are sorted into a final alphabetical order in which each slip appears under the heading marked no. 1, whether or not it is at the head

> 3 Door-Check, 21, 36, 92, 96
>
> 1 Check, Door-   *s/a* 2 Door
> 5 Rebate   4 Jamb
> 6 Set-back (Door)

of the slip. In the example above, for instance, the slip would now be filed under the heading 'Check, Door-'. After a final check to ensure that the slips are correctly sorted according to this method—a very necessary precaution, since sorting slips by this system is not as easy as sorting every slip by its heading —the entries are ready for typing. As soon as the first item on each slip has been typed a light check or tick is placed against it on the slip, which is then transferred immediately to the alphabetical position of the second item (if any). Thus, in the example given above, after an entry has been typed for:

Check, Door- *see* Door-Check

the slip will be transferred to the second item on the list, i.e. to the heading for Door. When this position is reached in the typing, the entry is typed for:

Door *see also* Door-Check

or, if there are no references under the word Door itself, in the average index an entry under the third item on the list—Door-Check—would probably prove sufficient since otherwise reference and actual entry would come together:

Door *see* Door-Check
Door-Check, 21, 36, 92, 96

which is an example of the kind of unnecessary entry which is best avoided. The slip is now transferred to the fourth heading, Jamb. When the last item has been reached and typed, the slip is resorted under the first heading (Check, Door-) ready for checking.

The advantages of this system are that it involves fewer slips to handle, eliminates variations in page-references under the various alternative headings, saves time in writing, maintains a closer control over headings and references and makes the manuscript index easier to use since it is not so unwieldy. There is little saving in time, however, since what is saved in writing entries is usually lost in the business of constantly resorting entries while typing. The resorting can however be prevented to a certain extent from interrupting the work of typing by resorting immediately only those items which involve the same or the next initial letter, the remainder being roughly sorted into four or five temporary bundles each covering a group of letters. The main resorting can then be left for a convenient interval such as when a page of typing has been completed. With a little practice the whole business can quickly be reduced to a routine which comes naturally and easily to the typist.

There are admittedly some disadvantages in using such a system. Its success depends on rigid consistency throughout: any deviation would be fatal to making a fool-proof index and much more wearisome checking would be necessary to ensure that no error had occurred. In the second place, it is not easy to estimate the total size of the index owing to the unequal number of entries on each slip so that—unless every item is counted in advance—some practice is necessary before the indexer can be sure that he is tailoring his index to a given length. Next, at no time is there a complete index in manuscript so that the indexer has to rely on the consistency of his own brain—aided of course by the testing of alternative headings—to make certain he has not used different headings for the same subject. This can be aided by making separate entry slips for references from synonyms. Finally, unless the indexer is his own typist, it is necessary to see to it that the typist thoroughly understands the system used, and is in no doubt concerning the alphabetisation of entries. From practical experience it has been found that the system is workable and that it does achieve what it sets out to do.

There are other ways of effecting economies in indexing which are not so elaborate and which may appeal to indexers who wish to speed up their work. One system that eliminates the rewriting of index entries to a large extent is dependent on the use of gummed sheets of paper perforated throughout their length at intervals of two or three inches. On these sheets the index entries are written or typed, one entry being made on each perforated strip. When the indexing is completed and the entries have been checked with the text the strips are separated at their perforations (those who have had any experience of the acquittance rolls used by the British Army Pay Office will recognise the resemblance to army methods) and sorted alphabetically. After this is done, a certain amount of editing is necessary to eliminate repetition of headings, duplication of references, etc., and then the slips are mounted on quarto rough paper backing. The index is now ready for the printer. There is naturally a slight wastage of stationery in using this method, since to maintain speed it is preferable to make fresh entries for each page reference to the same heading rather than to go back through previous pages to find the first mention of that heading. Against this there is the speed gained owing to the use of continuous stationery, the reduction of rewriting or retyping to a minimum, the elimination of the possibility of errors through copying page references, and the obviation of checking the typist's copy. If at the time of making the entries a carbon copy is made on unperforated paper, it then becomes possible to check the original entries against the text at any time, so that additions and corrections can be got ready by the time the proofs arrive from the printer. There is the additional advantage that during the greater part of the process the indexer is handling pages and not slips, an advantage which is very attractive to all but the card-index addict. It is a system which is much used in indexing periodicals since the indexing can be carried on throughout the year, afterthoughts occasioned by the contents of succeeding issues (such as the choice of an alternative heading for a new or controversial subject) being easy to insert owing to the fact that the slips are not separated until the current volume of the periodical is completed. Numbering each perforated page to correspond with the paging of the periodical adds to ease of reference. Gummed perforated paper of the type needed for this work can easily be obtained from any large stationer at a moderate cost.

Other short cuts to indexing are now being made possible by the introduction of modern office equipment. For instance,

some indexes—such as those of standard year books and directories—are not subject to very extensive variations from year
to year, though such alterations as are necessary are of course
of great importance. Here it is possible, except in the case of
very large indexes, to put all the entries on a visible index consisting of a series of metal flanged leaves bearing on each side
cellophane-covered stiff strips which slip into slots on either
margin. This is a most flexible type of index, for each side of
each metal leaf will hold up to two hundred entries, and insertions and withdrawals of individual entries can be made
immediately, provided that the column is not completely full.
The entries are written or typed on perforated sheets of paper
or thin cardboard and are only separated when ready for sorting
and insertion. The metal leaves can be supported on stands or
supplied in folding form for desk work, and each leaf can be
detached—a point which makes the index more mobile. As
against the comparatively high initial cost of this equipment,
subsequent expenditure is limited to renewal of stationery, since
none of the parts is likely to wear out or need repair.

Very large indexes of the semi-permanent type can be accommodated on a revolving drum supported and enclosed within a
case mounted on wheels. On the drum are holders which secure
the index cards and the drum can be flicked round at ease to
bring the correct file uppermost. This type of equipment is used
mainly in offices for records of customers, subscribers, etc., but
can easily be adapted for indexing requirements and is, in fact,
very suitable for indexing multi-volume works such as encyclopaedias, large legal or medical treatises, etc., since each drum
will hold two thousand cards, and the cards themselves, being
8 in. by 5 in., are large enough to allow for entering numerous
aspects of a general heading or a large number of references to
one subject on the same card.

For small indexes probably nothing can beat the thumb-
indexed loose-leaf holder. Each page can represent one letter
in the alphabet—or one large section of a letter—and entries
can be made in their approximate positions. When a page gets
too full or entries can no longer be given in any semblance of
order, it can be replaced by two new pages on which the entries
are rewritten, retyped or cut up and mounted in their correct
positions. Alternatively, the sheaf form of holder such as is still

used by some public libraries can be used. Here each entry is written on a separate slotted leaf and the leaves are held firmly by the margin by one or two metal rods which are locked in position by a simple key. When fresh indexing is being done the new slips are inserted loosely in their right places, checked for any error of placing, and then finally fixed in position at regular intervals—insertion one by one is usually uneconomical since the unlocking and locking of the sheaf holders, the lifting out and replacing of leaves, etc., takes an appreciable amount of time.

For very small indexes, where the publisher is able to allow only six or eight pages for the index, it is sometimes possible to write all the index entries for a page on the broad margin at the foot of the page proof. When the indexing is completed, the alphabetical order of the entries on a page is indicated by numbers and the same procedure followed as on pages 37–38. This has the advantage that the actual wording of the text can be compared when deciding on the final form of the index entries.

No progress in mechanisation can however eliminate the need for the indexer to read the material to be indexed carefully before starting work, and to give due consideration to the heading for each index entry. The most that can be done is to reduce the mechanical effort—writing, sorting, re-writing, typing, checking, etc.—as much as possible, and this will in turn help the indexer to carry out the process of indexing more thoroughly and more speedily.

Some
difficulties

'The English,' Herr Heinrich had said,
*'do not understand indexing. It is the root
of all good organisation.'*
　　　　　　　H. G. WELLS: Mr. Britling Sees
　　　　　　　　　　　　　　it Through

THE INDEXING OF NAMES and places is for the most part straightforward. There are, however, certain points on which difficulties are bound to arise, and it is essential to make clear-cut decisions on the method of procedure and to adhere to them throughout.

In the case of the names of people, the indexing of double-barrelled names is one point on which many indexers hesitate. If, for example, the name Albert Smith-Jones occurs, the question is whether the majority of readers will look for references to him under Smith or Jones. Some readers may not remember whether Smith is part of the surname or not; others will remember the whole of the double-barrelled name as though it were one word. The only satisfactory way of dealing with the problem is to make all the entries under one form of the name, and to refer from the form which it has been decided not to use:

Smith-Jones, Albert, 15, 63

Jones, Albert Smith-, *see* Smith-Jones, Albert

The main point is, that once having decided under which part the name is to be indexed, the same rule should be followed for all other double-barrelled names in the book, for the reader will naturally assume that such a procedure has been adopted and will resent any inconsistencies.

More difficulty is experienced with the names of titled people, especially those who have recently been honoured. In the case of titled people of the past, such as Disraeli, or Bacon, one form has now become almost universally accepted, so that it is not at all difficult to decide that only references are needed from Beaconsfield, or Verulam. But modern titles cause more difficulty: in the case, for example, of Lord Passfield, many people still remember him as Sidney Webb, while others will look for him under his title. It is reasonable to assume, however, that in the majority of cases a person will be remembered by the latest form of his name. The main point, however, is still consistency: the indexer should decide which form he is going to use, and then keep to his rule throughout. Occasionally this will produce a main entry under the less-known form of name, but this is more than offset by the assurance with which any reader can use the index quickly and accurately.

Married women who use both their own names and their husbands'—and perhaps their maiden names as well—should be dealt with in similar fashion:

Wainwright, Alice (*Mrs.* Robert Graham), 17, 32

Graham, *Mrs.* Robert, *see* Wainwright, Alice

The entries sometimes become more complicated, when a woman marries more than once, but the same principle should be followed:

Wainwright, Alice (*Mrs.* Robert Graham, *afterwards Mrs.* Arthur Randolph), 17, 32

Graham, *Mrs.* Robert, *see* Wainwright, Alice

Randolph, *Mrs.* Arthur, *see* Wainwright, Alice

A similar method can be followed in the case of other changes of name. For instance, the great bibliographer William Swan Sonnenschein changed his name to William Swan Stallybrass. The index entries would read:

Sonnenschein, William Swan (*afterwards* William Swan Stallybrass), 138, 149

Stallybrass, William Swan, *see* Sonnenschein, William Swan ·

In all entries of this kind, it is of service to readers to include the other forms of changes of name in the main entries, so that the reasons for reference from the other forms of the name are perfectly clear.

The names of organisations, government departments, etc., present difficulties from time to time. In the first place, the important word is rarely first in the name; thus, in the case of the Department of Education and Science, the important word is Education, and not everyone even nowadays can remember whether it is the Board or the Department or the Ministry of Education. The same applies to associations and societies, such as, for instance, the Institution of Electrical Engineers: not everyone can say for certain whether it is Institute or Institution, but everyone will remember the last part of the name. Here is a definite case for transposing the name, so that the majority of readers can find the main entry immediately:

Education and Science, Department of, 18, 97

Electrical Engineers, Institution of, 86

with the necessary references for those who look under the first word of the name:

> Department of Education and Science, *see*
> Education and Science, Department of
>
>> Institution of Electrical Engineers, *see*
>> Electrical Engineers, Institution of

In some cases it may be possible to make one reference do the work of several. For example, in a book containing many references to various government departments, a general reference can be made:

> Ministry. *For government departments whose names begin with this word, see under the names of the subjects with which they deal: e.g.,* Transport, Ministry of

and a similar method can be adopted for other types of organisation.

The names of commercial organisations must be treated carefully. Most are straightforward, but some present problems. The name, for instance, of one well-known publisher—Crosby Lockwood—is of course a straightforward example of forename and surname. Nevertheless, many people would be unable to say whether it is Crosby, Lockwood—i.e. the combination of the names of two partners—or otherwise. Similarly, such names as Freeman, Hardy and Willis, or Sears, Roebuck, all give cause for hesitation to some people when they have to look them up in a telephone directory. When there is any doubt in the mind of the indexer, a glance at the form or forms of entry in a commercial or telephone directory will help him to decide on the most useful forms for the reader.

The names of places also present difficulties occasionally. Many countries and cities, for instance, have changed their names in recent years: Abyssinia to Ethiopia, Palestine to Israel, Siam to Thailand, Constantinople to Istanbul, etc., and whatever form is used in the text of the book, the correct main entry for them in the index will generally be under the latest form, except where the text of the book differentiates between the two names. In any event, references should be made from former names:

Thailand, 7, 13, 18

Siam, *see* Thailand

Palestine, *see* Israel

Israel, 78, 92

There are also the places whose names are spelt in various ways: Beirût or Beyrout, Geneva or Genf, Göteborg, or Gothenburg, Praha or Prague, etc. Here the name is usually spelt in one way in the text, but the reader may first look for the name under a different spelling. It is therefore necessary to make the necessary references, and in constructing them—or foreseeing what alternatives may be used—it is a good rule to use a standard work of reference such as the *Statesman's Year-Book* (Macmillan, published annually), or Webster's *Geographical Dictionary* (Bell, latest edition).

Even with ordinary words there is occasionally room for doubt. For example, which should be used?—gaoler, jailer or jailor, palaeography or paleography, immunization or immunisation? With regard to the last two examples, the house style of the publisher who is publishing the book or the style of the printing house that is printing the book will finally determine which is used, but if the index is being prepared while the book is still in manuscript, it is as well to find out in advance exactly what the current policy is, since any alteration in spelling made thereby may throw out the order of entries as submitted in draft. The house style, which is merely the code of rules maintained by each publishing or printing house to ensure consistency and accuracy in all publications issued by it, is easily determinable from the proofs of the book as used for making the index. With regard to such words as inquiry and enquiry, it is a good rule to choose either the more conservative or the more modern form, and then to keep the same policy throughout the rest of the index. Unless this is done, the index will not present an appearance of uniformity.

Common usage changes over the course of years: wireless telegraphy first became wireless, and now it is more usually radio; gas and oil engines are more usually known as internal combustion engines; for years cinema and kinema each had their adherents, but the first has almost entirely superseded the second. The text of the book will naturally give the main guidance on which forms should be used, but the possibility of the reader's looking under any other forms not used should always be examined, and in any doubtful cases it is best to make one reference too many rather than one too few.

Another pitfall is the ambiguity of very common terms such as seal, which may be an animal, or an impressed piece of wax; as trusteeship, which may refer to the individual trusteeship of the type known in legal practice in Great Britain and the United States, or to the international aspect of controlling a country on behalf of the United Nations; or, as distemper which can be either a form of paint, or a disease. In the larger works the same term may be used in different senses in different parts of the text. When the index is being constructed it is essential to watch for traps of this kind, so that the reader may not be misled, and to differentiate between them in the index entries:

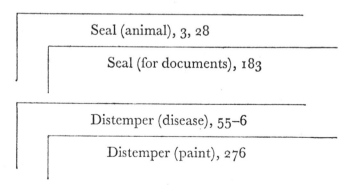

Seal (animal), 3, 28

Seal (for documents), 183

Distemper (disease), 55–6

Distemper (paint), 276

Fortunately, such points do not arise very much in the average small book, but in any work of an encyclopaedic character—

such as *Mrs. Beeton*—or one which covers a large number of subjects—such as the index to a general type of almanack as *Whitaker's*—the possibility of creating howlers by neglecting to watch for terms of this kind is always present.

The prefixes to surnames are also confusing. In British and American surnames there are not many difficulties: most people, for example, remember such names as De La Mare or Dos Passos almost as one word, and it is best to treat them as such, with the necessary references:

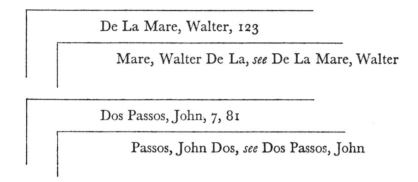

De La Mare, Walter, 123

Mare, Walter De La, *see* De La Mare, Walter

Dos Passos, John, 7, 81

Passos, John Dos, *see* Dos Passos, John

But note:

De Cournos, John, *see* Cournos

Cournos, John de, 14, 56

But in the case of foreign names, readers usually remember the name without the prefix, if it is a simple one. Thus few people think of Balzac as De Balzac, or Maupassant as De Maupassant. Even so, difficulties do occur, especially with such names as Salvador de Madariaga, Ten Brink, Villa Lobos, etc, and with most oriental names. The best method is to adopt the practice of one standard work of reference, such as Chambers's *Biographical Dictionary*, or Hyamson's *Biographical Dictionary*, or Webster's *Biographical Dictionary*, and to adhere to its general rules of entry for those names which are not included. For con-

D

temporary British and international names the current edition of *Who's Who* (Black, published annually) will not only give excellent guidance on the form of name to be used, but will also supply alternative forms for references. Where the index includes names of people from a very great number of countries, or where the indexer finds difficulty in establishing what is local usage, the very fine name indexes in *Keesing's Contemporary Archives* will be found of the greatest help—particularly in the indexing of Middle East, African, and Asian names. This major news summary can be consulted in any good reference library.

Some more
difficulties

*Time is of more value than type, and the
wear and tear of the temper than an extra
page of index.*

R. H. BUSK

EACH BOOK IS A PROBLEM in itself and needs to be approached
as an individual task: that is why there can never be a mechanical method of constructing its index. If there was, it could be
carried out in the same way that a ledger clerk enters up the
accounts of his firm. But in indexing, the indexer must have
sufficient knowledge and experience of the subject to make good
decisions on behalf of future readers, and he must have sufficient
imagination to be able to see the book and its index from the
points of view and the problems of all kinds of readers. Whenever a reader fails to find some piece of information which is
contained in the book, the indexer has failed in a portion of his
task.

The difference between a worthwhile and a poor index is
immense. A glance at the reviews in any reputable journal will
show how often reviewers complain of inadequate or unreliable
indexes which add a few pages to the text without elucidating
it fully. The responsibility for compiling an index involves some
research if the task is to be performed thoroughly. For instance,
the writer of the book may refer to a painter or an engineer by
his surname only. It is the indexer's duty to identify the person
mentioned, and to supply the full name or at least the initials
in order to make an adequate entry. If the writer refers merely
to Dumas, the indexer must make an entry under Dumas,
Alexandre, *père*, or under Dumas, Alexandre, *fils*, accordingly,
if he is to help the reader who wishes to know which is mentioned
without unnecessary reference to the text. The indexer should
visualise the book as one of many on the same subject on the
same group of shelves: the research worker will glance at them
all very quickly in order to determine which are relevant to his

work. A poor reference may prevent his making any use of that particular book, even though it may contain the very information he needs. In these days there is little time to waste in doing the indexer's work for him.

The research which the indexer carries out may produce much information of value as well as revealing inconsistencies. For example, where a term is used with which the indexer is unfamiliar, he will turn to the reference books on the subject to determine its exact meaning. In doing so, synonyms are revealed which may be more familiar to the reader and for which entries or references must be made, and perhaps different uses of the word which must be clearly distinguished. This knowledge he must contrive to pass on to the reader. Thus, if the name Newport is given in a book, the indexer will discover in identifying it that it may refer to different towns in different chapters. He will then distinguish between them in his index entries:

Newport (Monmouth), 181, 183

Newport (Isle of Wight), 76

or perhaps the word piscina is used in two different senses:

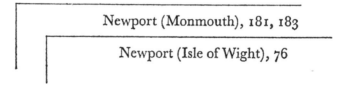

Piscina (fishpond), 98

Piscina (sacred basin), 132

The additions of dates and descriptions of people who might otherwise be confused with other persons of the same name is of definite service, especially in historical works where many people of the same name (and perhaps family) may occur during the course of centuries:

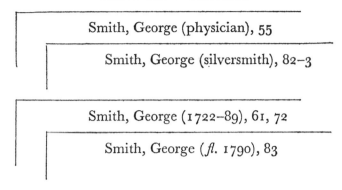

Smith, George (physician), 55

Smith, George (silversmith), 82–3

Smith, George (1722–89), 61, 72

Smith, George (*fl.* 1790), 83

In the same way, periodicals and newspapers should be identified by place of publication and date, since the same name may have been used for different journals in different places or in different centuries—or, what is more confusing, almost contemporary with each other:

Recorder (London, 1710–12), 143

Recorder (Newcastle, 1859–98), 71

and similar methods of identification should be used wherever there is the slightest chance of doubt or ambiguity.

It is customary to omit definite and indefinite articles at the beginning of an entry to facilitate arrangement and avoid confusion (since readers hardly ever remember the article accurately), but if the indexer feels that their omission will cause difficulty or will appear curious, they can be transposed:

Times, The, 22, 34

Temps, Le, 66

Foreign words and phrases are in fact subject to the same rules as those for English words. Occasional difficulties occur when letters appear which have no exact English equivalent, such as ä, ö, ü, ç, ñ, å, etc. In most instances these have a separate position in the alphabets of their own languages, but to give them an equivalent position in the index would mean that most readers would overlook them. It is best, therefore, to treat them as the simple letters a, o, u, etc., with reference from ae, oe, ue, etc., in the correct position.

In these days abbreviations are taking an increasingly important part in daily usage. Such abbreviations as UNESCO, USSR, FAO, etc., are so familiar that their full titles are not always accurately known. Each item must be considered on its individual merits. To take as examples those already mentioned, UNESCO and FAO are best entered under their abbreviations, with references from their full names and related headings:

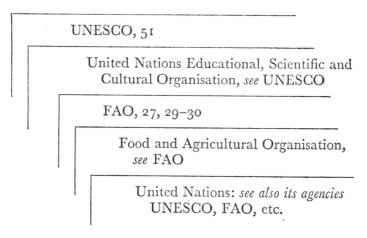

> UNESCO, 51
>
> United Nations Educational, Scientific and Cultural Organisation, *see* UNESCO
>
> FAO, 27, 29–30
>
> Food and Agricultural Organisation, *see* FAO
>
> United Nations: *see also its agencies* UNESCO, FAO, etc.

The USSR is a different problem. Most readers will think more readily of Russia or the Soviet Union and therefore the entries are best made as follows:

> Russia, 97–108
>
> USSR, *see* Russia
>
> Soviet Union, *see* Russia
>
> SSSR, *see* Russia

In all cases of abbreviations and acronyms they should be placed at the beginning of the alphabet:

FAO, 27, 29–30
FBI, 61
Fats, 83
Feeding-stuffs, 97
Fertilisers, 131

In some books, especially mathematical and scientific books, it may be necessary to enter symbols such as π, ∞, χ, $\neq$, etc. Where there are word equivalents, the solution is to enter them under those words with the symbol added in brackets:

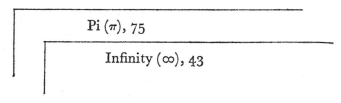

Pi (π), 75

Infinity (∞), 43

but where it is necessary to give entries for the symbols them-selves, it is best to enter them after the last word of the alphabet, and to add a note, indicating this, at the head of the index.

Half the secret of good indexing is the selection of the right subject-headings. The more practice in indexing, the greater the skill in selecting subject-headings and the greater the possi-bility of selecting exactly the right one. In the following passage from pages 54–55 of the late Dr. S. C. Bradford's *Documentation* (Crosby Lockwood, 1953), notes have been added in the margin similar to those which an indexer would enter as he read through the book:

Documentation.
purpose

The purpose of documentation. While library technique was still in the process of de-velopment, scientific man had already found it necessary to consider how to deal with the growing mass of individual papers published in the Transactions of Societies and independent Journals: papers record-ing original investigations, and, therefore, constituting the foundation on which fur-ther progress must be based. These papers needed cataloguing just as much, or even more, than books, which only record a summary of original discovery, after the pioneers are many years ahead.

Periodicals, Scientific, *indexing*

Perhaps the first suggestion to prepare a comprehensive catalogue of the whole of scientific periodical literature was made to

British Association
Henry, *Prof.*

the British Association in 1855, by Professor Henry of Washington. Eventually the suggestion first bore fruit in the pro-

R. Society. *Cat. of scientific papers*
Cat. of sci. papers
Index to foreign sci. periodicals
Patent Office. *Index to foreign sci. periodicals*

duction of the 'Catalogue of Scientific Papers' published by the Royal Society' from 1867 onwards. Simultaneously the 'Index to foreign scientific periodicals contained in the Patent Office Library' began to appear. The Royal Society's Catalogue is still in progress. Unfortunately the Patent Office Index ceased to appear with the volume for 1872. It is interesting to observe that the same ideas were involved in the preparation of these catalogues of papers as were seen in the earliest catalogues of books. For, while the Royal Society's Catalogue was arranged alphabetically under authors, the Patent Office Library's

Classification

Index was classified.

Even before the Royal Society's Catalogue, however, the output of scientific periodical literature had increased so much that it had become impossible for a scientific man to digest even all the literature of his own branch of knowledge, and so keep up to date within it. A new type of

Abstracts
Periodicals. *abstracts*

periodical was needed, which should survey broad fields of knowledge and summarize all important current papers in those fields, thus providing a bird's-eye view of progress. The earliest to appear of

Pharmaceutisches Centralblatt

this type of periodical was the *Pharmaceutisches Centralblatt* (afterwards *Chemisches*

Chemisches Zentral-
blatt

Zentralblatt), which commenced in 1830 and continues to this day.

This first 'abstracting periodical' was succeeded in the course of time by many others, covering definite fields of science and giving either abstracts of the current papers, short annotations or even merely *Quarterly Jnl. of the* references to them. Of such were the *Chemical Society* Quarterly Journal of the Chemical Society Chemical Society. (now British Abstracts), which began in *Qu. Jnl.* 1847, the *Zoological Record*, 1864, and on-*British Abstracts* wards, and the *Engineering Index*, commenc-*Zoological Record* ing in 1884. All these are still in progress.
Engineering Index

So were developed, side by side, a set of abstracting periodicals, providing summaries of individual current papers and the Royal Society's comprehensive catalogue, by authors, giving only titles of them all.

In the margin have been entered preliminary notes for index entries, as they might occur ro the indexer as he scans each page. In the first paragraph an entry must be made for 'Documentation—*purpose*', and others under 'Cataloguing—*periodicals*' and under 'Periodicals—*cataloguing*' would appear desirable. As the whole book deals with similar subjects, it is advisable to state the aspects of the subjects immediately, since otherwise too many entries will appear under the same general headings. Indeed, in any case it is best to give entries under the most specific headings in all cases, since it is certain that at least some of the readers will look under the specific headings, and others under the more general headings from which references should be made. Thus one reader in seeking material on Electrical Engineering will look under Engineering, while another will turn straight to Electrical Engineering. It will be noticed that alternative headings, such as Abstracts and Periodicals—*abstracts*, have been made throughout. When making the slips, the indexer will treat both of these as main headings for the time being, leaving till the index is completed the question of whether one of these should be made a 'see' reference to the other.

In the second paragraph the main subject is the indexing of scientific periodicals, and the appropriate entries should be made:

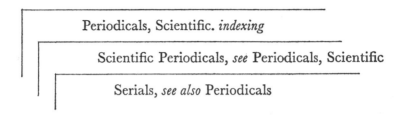

Periodicals, Scientific. *indexing*

Scientific Periodicals, *see* Periodicals, Scientific

Serials, *see also* Periodicals

an entry being made for Serials, since many people interested in the subject will turn directly to this word which denotes not only Periodicals, but also the Transactions and Proceedings of Societies, year books, and other items issued from time to time under the same title. An entry must also be made for Professor Henry, and for this purpose some little research should be made to discover his forenames or initials from such sources as the *Dictionary of American Biography*. Then, entries must be made under the individual periodicals and their issuing bodies:

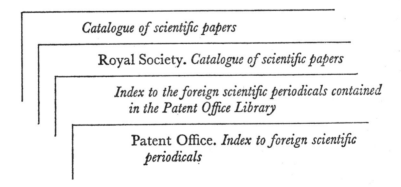

Catalogue of scientific papers

Royal Society. *Catalogue of scientific papers*

Index to the foreign scientific periodicals contained in the Patent Office Library

Patent Office. *Index to foreign scientific periodicals*

and to these the dates of commencement and decease must be added, when these have been checked with standard reference works such as Gregory's *Union List of Serials* (New York, H. W. Wilson) and its successors.

In indexing, there are always some points which do not require entries. For instance, in the first paragraph the phrase

'Transactions of Societies and independent Journals' needs no entries, and in the second no index entry is needed for 'Washington' or for 'catalogues of books'. In the fourth, 'annotations' wants no entry. The only test is, whether any purpose is served in making such entries. If an index entry is unlikely to give the reader any help, then none need be made.

In the third paragraph, there is need only for entries for the periodicals mentioned:

> *Pharmaceutisches Centralblatt,* 16–17
>
> > *Chemisches Zentralblatt,* 17

and similarly for the fourth paragraph. But in the case of the *Engineering Index,* the investigation undertaken to determine its dates will reveal that it is the publication of a society, and the entries will therefore be:

> *Engineering Index,* 17
>
> > American Society of Mechanical Engineers.
> > *Engineering Index,* 17
> >
> > > Mechanical Engineers, American Society of.
> > > *see* American Society of Mechanical Engineers

and similar circumstances may be discovered as other periodicals are investigated. In the fifth paragraph, an entry for 'Royal Society' is unnecessary.

Care should be taken to avoid useless entries. For example, had the phrase occurred: 'In this catalogue no mention is made of the Royal Society', it would be wrong to make an entry for the Royal Society. Negative references of this kind are the very type of problem which prove that indexing is no mechanical art which could safely be left to a clerical worker with instructions to index every mention of proper names, and so on.

Nevertheless, this does not mean that any part of the book should remain unconsidered from the point of view of the reader. The indexer must constantly keep in mind the requirements of the many readers who wish to refer again to something only imperfectly remembered. It may be that the very idea they are seeking may have been mentioned in the preface, or in the caption below an illustration. It may be that the reader remembers the title of a chapter, the name of a man mentioned only in a foreword, or in a footnote, or a table in an appendix. Even the names of the people mentioned in prefaces, bibliographies, illustrations, footnotes, and all ideas put forward in these items, should be included, and the index should truly represent the whole book.

One of the great problems of indexing is the difficulty of deciding between the relative importance of geographical position and subject. For example, if a description of the types of cultivated flowers to be found in the Scilly Isles is given in a book on modern trades, should the entry be made under 'Scilly Isles' or under 'flowers'? The only satisfactory method of dealing with this problem is to make double entry:

Scilly Isles. *flowers*, 77–89

Flowers. *Scilly Isles*, 77–89

On the other hand, if this description appeared in a book on the Scilly Isles, it would only be necessary to make an entry under 'Flowers', and if it appeared in a book on the cultivation of flowers, there would only be need for an entry under 'Scilly Isles'.

In phrasing headings for entries it is well to determine in advance whether these shall be in the plural or in the singular, as a general rule. For example, in a book on different kinds of trees, should one put:

Birch	*or*	Birches
Elm		Elms
Fir		Firs
Larch		Larches
Oak		Oaks

A brief glance will show that the singular is more attractive and less clumsy. In some cases it may be preferable to use the plural, but the main point is to attempt to maintain consistency throughout.

There are two forms of reference: the 'see' reference and the 'see also' reference. They have very different uses. The 'see' reference is used for referring the reader from alternative forms of entry to the one under which the page reference will be found:

Costume, 89, 91–6

Dress, *see* Costume

The 'see also' reference, on the other hand, is made from main entries to associated subjects. For instance, in addition to the mention of costume in general, it might be necessary to refer the reader to additional entries under shoes and gloves:

Costume, 89, 91–6
see also names of individual articles
of apparel: Gloves, Shoes, etc.

It is customary to make these 'see also' references from general subjects to specific subjects, but not from specific subjects back to general subjects, for this would be just that kind of vicious circle which Stephen Leacock has so rightly attacked, Thus, in the example just given, it would not be necessary to make entries: Gloves, *see also* Costume; or Shoes, *see also* Costume. The principle is sound, for the reader who is seeking information on Gloves, will not usually need to be reminded of other articles of costume, which is the purpose of the 'see also' reference. On the other hand, 'see also' references are always desirable for associated subjects of similar and possibly equal importance:

Radio, *see also* Television

Television, *see also* Radio

Here 'see also' references have been given each way, for television is not a branch of radio, but rather a parallel subject, so that readers will need to be reminded that entries which may also interest them appear under the other heading as well.

Some
economies
in indexing

*I certainly think that the best book in the
world would owe the most to a good index,
and the worst book, if it had but a single,
good thought in it, might be kept alive
by it.*

HORACE BINNEY: To S. Austin
Allibone, 8 April 1868

IT IS RARE THAT as much space is available as the author would
like for his index. This will limit the number of references which
can be made, but there are certain economies which can without detriment be made, and which will allow the indexer safely
to make more entries in the same amount of space.

One of the most usual economies, and one which can be
effected without detriment to the average medium-size index,
is the combination of subjects with the operations associated
with them. For example, in a book on finance, there may be
several references to Banks, and several more to the practice of
Banking. If there is a large number of references to both of
these it will necessary to make separate references, but if
there are only a few it should be considered whether these two
could safely be combined under the one heading Banks and
Banking. If it is considered that this will be no hindrance to
the reader, the combination should certainly be made, and thus
one line will take the place of two:

$$\left.\begin{array}{l}\text{Banking, 56, 69}\\\text{Banks, 58, 68}\end{array}\right\} = \text{Banks and Banking, 56, 58, 68, 69}$$

Other such headings as Ploughs and Ploughing, Hotels and
Hotel Keeping, Print and Printing, etc., will immediately occur
to the reader. Where, however, the combination appears at all
forced, as for example, Dress and Dressmaking, it should be
avoided. Such combinations depend too on the similarity

between the two terms: in the case of Horses and Riding, for instance, little is gained, for even if the combination of the two were made under the heading Horses and Horseriding, it would still be necessary to make a reference from Riding, whereas in the case of Banks and Banking, a reference from Banking is unnecessary in a fairly small index in which the reader looking for Banking would immediately see the word under Banks.

Another system of combination—and one which is in any case advisable—is that of synonyms and antonyms. Obvious examples are Peace and War, Employment and Unemployment, Heat and Cold, etc. Pairs of terms such as these are so closely related that, except in works especially devoted to their detailed discussion, it is best to combine the references for the benefit of the reader, who is probably interested in hearing both sides of the question. It will still be necessary to make references from the terms not used, but space will be saved wherever the entries under the alternative forms would themselves have exceeded one line. For this purpose, it is best to keep close at hand a good dictionary of synonyms and antonyms (such as Roget's *Thesaurus*) to help in the choice of suitable combinations.

In some cases it may be more economical from the point of view of the reader to use added entries rather than references. For instance, in the case where Agriculture is mentioned only two or three times in a book, the entries would read:

> Agriculture, 17, 26
> Farming, *see* Agriculture

In this case, the reference could just as well be made a full entry:

> Agriculture, 17, 26
> Farming, 17, 26

since no more space is occupied thereby, and the time of the reader is saved. Moreover, in the longer 'see' references of this kind, a line may be saved here and there.

On the other hand, a watch should be kept for near-synonymous entries of this kind, wherever the substitution of a 'see' reference could save space:

> Illumination, 77, 86–9, 91, 94–8
> Light, 77, 86–9, 91, 94–8, 101–20

in which there is a case where a reference 'Light, *see* Illumination', and a combination of the page-references broken up under aspects, would be justified. It is not usually possible to judge whether amendments of this kind are advisable until the index entries are completed, and it is best to follow ordinary practice while actually indexing, and not to attempt adjustments of this kind until the situation can be sized up from the complete entries. Further economy can be achieved by the use of an oblique stroke:

abstract/abstractions
banks/banking

The arrangement of the contents of complicated entries and especially of the aspects of subjects may have much bearing on the amount of space used for the index. Consider the relative merits of the following example, which is set out in two different ways:

Fox-tail-Grass, 324; Alpine, 333; Marsh (Bent-stemmed) 332; Meadow, 332; Orange-anthered, 333; Slender, 332; Tuberous, 333	Fox-tail-Grass, 324
	Alpine, 333
	Marsh (Bent-stemmed), 332
	Meadow, 332
	Orange-anthered, 333
	Slender, 332
	Tuberous, 333
Hair-Grass, 326; Alpine, 336; Bog, 336; Crested, 327, 338; Early, 337; Grey, 326, 336; Heath (Wavy), 336; Silvery, 337; Tufted, 336	Hair-Grass, 326
	Alpine, 336
	Bog, 336
	Crested, 327, 338
	Early, 337
	Grey, 326 336
	Heath (Wavy), 336
	Silvery, 337
	Tufted, 336

The left-hand setting saves at least six lines in a comparatively small number of entries, but at the cost of some legibility. The author must weigh this question of ease of reference against the possibility of including more references. In some cases, the choice between the two types of setting is straightforward: the right-hand setting is particularly suitable for scientific and technical books, where the reader wishes to refer quickly to a particular species or specific item. On the other hand, the left-hand setting is frequently used for biographical and historical material, where such entries form a brief outline of events or of a man's life in semi-narrative form, and can be read as such. In the more detailed scientific indexes the right-hand setting must be maintained, in order to show the relation of aspects to each other, as in the following example:

> Milk
> > boiled, 187, 355
> > certified, 184–5
> > > bottled, 184
> > > in bulk, 185
> > clean, 153, 157, 185
> > condensed, 101, 161, 185
> Molasses, 197
> Mustard, 237

It is true that the elimination of aspects, and the massing of references under the main headings, would save a great amount of space, but this would not be a justifiable economy. The ease of the reader must always be uppermost in all consideration of short-cuts and economies, and his time will not be saved if he has to look up many references in order to discover that which deals with the particular aspect in which he is interested. In fact, the more that complicated entries can be divided up by their aspects, the better. This will still involve the inclusion of additional entries—or at least references—under the aspects; in the example just given, for instance, additional entries would be made:

> Boiled milk, 187, 355
> Certified milk, 184–5
> Clean milk, 153, 157, 185
> > etc. etc.

There are other economies which can be made, such as the employment of smaller type, the elimination of leading, the decrease in the amount of space allotted to indentation, the planning of three columns of index per page, etc., but these are all considerations which are the province of the printer and the publisher, and the author can do little to influence decisions in these matters. But he can and should attempt to find out in advance what these decisions are, for each has some bearing on the way in which he frames his headings. And at the same time he can help considerably by his concise and careful choice of headings, and by his adoption of some of the expedients described in this chapter.

How Boolean
can your
index be?[1]

We know that in the construction of a good index, there is far more scope for the exercise of judgment and abilities, than is commonly supposed. We feel the merits of the compiler of such an index, and we are very ready to testify our thankfulness for his exertions.

DR. SAMUEL AUSTIN ALLIBONE:
Critical Dictionary of Authors

IN THE FINAL EDITING of an index before it is sent to the printers one of the great problems is ensuring that all the references are tied up satisfactorily. It is essential to make sufficient references from general subjects (such as Commerce, Agriculture, etc.) to their branches (Exports and Imports, etc., in the case of Commerce; Cattle, Dairy Farming, etc., in the case of Agriculture, etc.), and to make certain that subjects which overlap with two or more other subjects are provided with references from all the topics involved. Sometimes the relation between subjects is rather complicated so that it is difficult to see the wood for the trees, and in this connection the application of Boolean algebra can often prove of great help to the indexer.

George Frederick Boole, a leading nineteenth-century mathematician, made a substantial contribution to current understanding of the relationship of one subject to another by demonstrating that such relationships are subject to algebraical laws. Without going into the mathematical aspects of the subject to more than a superficial extent, it is still possible to apply Boole's conclusions to advantage in modern indexing. Take, for example, the simplest case in which two subjects

[1] In spite of the menacing appearance of the diagrams no knowledge of mathematics is needed to understand this short chapter. Nevertheless, those with an especial distaste for mathematics can safely pass on to the next chapter, since this is simply one of the many different methods of approaching the problem of indexing.

partly overlap: this in Boolean algebra can be depicted by the following diagram in which the two subjects A and x are shown by unequal ovals though the area is in fact unimportant:

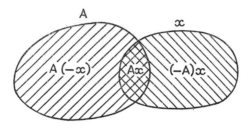

In this diagram A(–x) represents all the area of the subject A which does not overlap with x, and Ax represents all the overlapping area of the two subjects. Now it is clear that reference must be made from both subjects A and x to Ax, but that it is not necessary to make references to Ax from A(–x) or from (–A)x. Suppose A represents the subject Commerce and x National Revenue, while Ax indicates such aspects as Customs and Excise Duties, reference will be made from both Commerce and National Revenue to Customs and Excise Duties; but if A(–x) includes such subjects as Docks, Shipping, etc., while (–A)x includes Income Tax, Entertainments Tax, etc., reference will not be necessary from any in A(–x) to any in (–A)x.

If this was as far as Boolean algebra went, its application would be unnecessarily cumbersome in ordinary indexing. Its real worth comes in the more complicated case. Take, for instance, the case of five interconnected subjects:

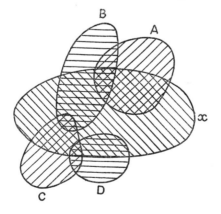

This case is sufficiently complex for its depiction graphically to simplify the problem of references for the indexer to a considerable extent. Thus it is clear that the subjects A, B, C and D are all related in some way to x, and that A, B, C and D are interconnected in themselves, though D is only remotely connected with A through B and C and, in fact, is more directly related with A through x. If the diagram is thought of as representing three-dimensional objects in which A, B, C and D are spheres intersecting with each other and with the vast mass x, the representation of real subjects becomes more vivid.

Suppose x represents Agriculture, and A, B, C and D represent the subjects Farm Buildings, Fencing, Gates, and Cattle respectively, it will be seen that each subject overlaps with the next to some extent. Again, A (Farm Buildings) and D (Cattle) have a direct relationship through the main subject Agriculture, although the connection of D (Cattle) through C (Gates), and B (Fencing) is also apparent. Thus the references would be made:

> Agriculture
>   *see also* Cattle, Farm Buildings, Fencing, Gates, etc.
> Fencing
>   *see also* Gates
> Gates (Farming)
>   *see also* Cattle
> Farm Buildings
>   *see also* Cattle, Dairies, Fencing, Silos, etc.

but reverse references from Cattle, Farm Buildings, etc., to Agriculture, would of course be unnecessary.

The problem of the subject-within-a-subject is of particular interest, though it may well delay the indexer whenever it occurs. In graphical form, one such problem can be shown as:

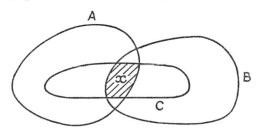

in which the subject C is partly included in both A and B, while A and B are themselves overlapping topics. Points of especial interest are that no part of C is outside both A and B, and that in one small area x (indicated here by shading) A, B, and C all overlap—that is, they all have a limited area of common interests. Thus if A represents the Theatre, B represents Television, while C is Stage Representation of Drama, the shaded area x may be taken to indicate the Televising of Stage Performances. Now here references will be necessary from A to C, from B to C, and from B direct to x because of the technical problems involved—whereas the approach of A to x may well be made through C. Thus the references would be made:

Theatre
    see also Drama (Stage Performances); Television
Television
    see also Drama (Stage Performances); Televised Theatre;
        Theatre
Drama (Stage Performances)
    see also Televised Theatre

References in this case are made from Theatre to Television and from Television to Theatre, since they are connected subjects, but neither is subordinate to the other.

A different form of overlapping which frequently occurs in indexing may be shown graphically as follows:

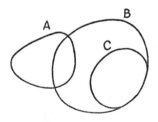

Here we have two overlapping subjects, one of which wholly includes a fringe subject within its field. It will be seen that A and C have no relationship whatever beyond C's connection with a part of A through B. C is deliberately shown on the far side of B to denote its very distant relationship to A. Let us assume that A represents Locomotives, B Railways and C

Station Restaurants. It will be seen that references will be needed on these lines:

Railways
  see also Locomotives; Station Restaurants, etc.
Locomotives
  see also Railways

Thus a reference is made from Locomotives to Railways since Locomotives is a subject which has other aspects than those connected with Railways. On the other hand, no reference is made from Station Restaurants to Locomotives though, in fact, the user of the index will be reminded of the existence of references in the text to Station Restaurants when he turns from Locomotives to the heading Railways.

How far is all this necessary? In straightforward indexing very little; but whenever the indexer is considering securing the inter-relationship of large general headings to the many partly interlocking topics which may occur throughout the text, a rough diagram on these lines may well help him to grasp the whole hierarchical structure and to ensure that no important reference is overlooked.

Chain indexing

A poor index perpetrates a kind of literary fraud.

JED H. TAYLOR:
Books with no indexes

IN THE DIFFICULT TASK of adequately indexing subjects and ideas, the indexer needs all the help he can get if he is to make a thorough job of his index. In this connection, the work of librarians and bibliographers in developing the principles of chain indexing may be found to illuminate many troublesome areas where the indexer is so closely involved that he cannot see the wood for the trees. Chain indexing, originally put forward as an aid to the indexing of book classifications by the great Indian librarian, Dr. S. R. Ranganathan, has since been elaborated and adapted to western bibliographical needs by several British librarians and organisations, notably the staff of the *British national bibliography*. The fundamental aim of chain indexing is to ensure that each concept is linked to its direct relations by utilising an almost mechanical process of checking its position in the hierarchy of the subject and making certain that these links in the 'chain' are indexed. In this way it is hoped that the users of the index will not fail to find the entry they need just because they omit to look under the most specific subject they have in mind.

Thus, the classification of invertebrates may be shown as follows:

Invertebrates
Protozoa
Mesozoa
Parazoa
Metazoa
Mollusca and molluscoidea

73

Other invertebrates
  Wormlike animals
  Arthropoda
  Onychophora
  Progoneata
  Opisthogoneata
  Symphyla
  Pauropoda
  Insecta
    Synaptera
    Orthoptera
    etc., etc.

If, therefore, the subject to be indexed is Locusts (which are classified under the last item, i.e. Orthoptera), the indexer of a classification scheme will make certain that the enquirer discovers the entry for Locusts by including references to:

Invertebrates
Insects
Orthoptera

since any of these three references will lead the searcher straight to the very classification tables which include an entry for Locusts. This system is obviously of great use in book classification, and in searching for bibliographical references (since a work on one of the larger groups may well include a considerable section on the more specific subject desired), but its direct applications to general indexing are more limited.

Where it is of great value is in the editing of indexes to highly detailed works on the more recondite subjects. Here the indexer may have done his job meticulously without feeling at all sure that he has fully covered all the aspects and accepted terminology of his subject so that a reader, looking for parallel references to works he has already consulted, will not overlook material of interest in the book in hand.

Take for example the indexing of a work on psychology in general. Here is a field where the terminology varies greatly and is constantly developing. The following summary of the relevant Dewey Decimal classification tables used in so many libraries today gives some idea of the complicated nature of the subject and its many facets:

> Psychology
>> applied psychology
>>> functionalism
>>> reductionism
>>>> behaviourism
>>>> reflexology
>>>>> Pavlov's theory of behaviour
>>> psychoanalytic systems
>>>> Freud
>>>> Adler
>>>> Jung
>>>> etc., etc.

Thus, the indexer confronted with the necessity of making certain that a passage on the psychology of reflex actions was not overlooked, would do well to glance at the appropriate tables of the Dewey Decimal Classification (or, if he wishes, those of the Library of Congress Classification) and there ascertain that, in addition to an entry under reflex actions—and, if relevant, under Pavlov or Thorndike—there could well be references from:

> behaviourism
> *and* reductionism

and that it would be important to see that any entries under psychology or applied psychology also drew attention (even by a general reference) to the more specific references he had already made.

The reassurance to the indexer that can be obtained by studying and following the procedure adopted in this field by bibliographers is too important to be set aside as partially irrelevant to the day-to-day work of book- or periodical-indexing. Thus, a study of the literature on the subject can make the indexer's task less tedious and much more thorough (and interesting). In this connection, the reader is recommended to study three articles: Jack Mill's 'Chain indexing and the classified catalogue' and D. W. Doughty's 'Chain procedure subject indexing and featuring a classified catalogue' in volume

57 of the *Library Association Record* (April 1955, pages 141–8; and, May 1955, pages 173–8, respectively); and, E. J. Coates's 'The use of *BNB* in dictionary cataloguing' in volume 59 of the *Library Association Record* (June 1957, pages 197–202). Sets of this periodical will be found in all university and public libraries.

Fees for indexing

THE QUESTION OF WHAT is a fair charge for indexing is often raised, and it is one which is extremely difficult to answer to anyone's satisfaction. Certainly if indexing was charged at its true rate few indexes would ever be commissioned. The process of indexing is in fact a long and tedious business: if a record is kept of every moment spent on indexing a book and the work is analysed, the indexer who is new to his work may be very surprised. For indexing, say, an historical work of some 420 pages the total time spent may well prove to be something like this:

		hours
a)	preliminary rapid reading of text	3
b)	reading text and marking passages for index entries	7
c)	copying entries out on index slips	6
d)	sorting, arranging, editing, etc., slips	4
e)	typing index for 8-page index	3
f)	final checking of typescript with slips	1
g)	proof-reading: galley- and page-proofs	3
		27 hours

Admittedly some indexes will be made faster than others and, with experience, it may be possible to reduce these figures slightly, but it is still unlikely that the total time spent on making a good 8-page index will amount to less than twenty hours. To take the individual processes separately:

    a) preliminary rapid reading is essential if the indexer is to do justice to the book: he must have a general idea of what the book is about.

b) ⎱ it is possible to combine these two processes—in fact, many
c) ⎰ experienced indexers do so as a matter of course, but this
      may well have the effect of adding to rather than reducing
      the number of hours spent on this aspect, since there are
      really three processes involved. These are: consideration
      of whether an index entry is necessary, selection of suitable
      headings and references, and the actual clerical work—all
      calling for some adaptability of mind.

d) the time allowed is barely sufficient for a thorough job,
      for editing very often involves considerable alteration of
      subject headings, references, etc.

e) ⎱ these are entirely dependent on the individual typist and
f) ⎰ the system of checking—the work can be farmed out, but
      the indexer's reward is then much less if (as he must, owing
      to the nature of the work) he uses a good secretarial
      service.

g) again, a bare minimum is allowed for fast and thorough
      checking.

The figures given above relate to the indexing of a purely
general type of book such as any intelligent person with good
general knowledge might be prepared to attempt. Where a
highly technical work is concerned the time taken by every one
of these items is likely to increase—in the more difficult cases to
almost double, especially if foreign or highly-specialised words
and terms occur frequently throughout the text.

What, then, is a reasonable reward for indexing at the present
time? If the charge is based on the work done in the examples
given above, we can assume that the indexing of a purely
general work represents half a week's work (i.e. three days each
of eight hours), and that of a technical work a full week's work.
Assuming that such work, if carried out full time, would be
paid at the rate of £2,000 a year, the basic cost of indexing a
general work of about 400 pages would be about £20 and of
a technical book of the same length about £40, to which must
be added an agreed percentage if the work is carried out at
home, or if the indexer supplies his own materials.

These figures would not appear to be unreasonable, and
probably most publishers would not object to such charges if
they were able to get good indexes for their money. The ob-

jections are in fact most likely to come from the indexers themselves, who will point out that many more hours may have to be
given proportionately to quite short indexes. This can arise in a
number of ways. First, a book may be very difficult to index
owing to its contents: it may be highly technical, or it may be
written in such a way that the meaning of particular sentences
or phrases may be hard to grasp—the indexing of Wittgen-
stein's famous *Tractatus Logico-philosophicus* would come under
this heading. Alternatively, the reason may be from a purely
mechanical cause: as is quite usual, the publisher may have
decided in advance that only a certain number of pages can be
allocated to the index. Now, it is a curious fact that the smaller
the index to any large volume the greater the problem for the
indexer—that is, if he is to produce a real index and not an
apology for one. The difficulty lies in selecting from a mass of possible entries those of sufficient importance to justify inclusion in
the limited space available. The justice of this will especially be
recognised in the particular case of periodicals where some
form of selective indexing is almost always inevitable. Thus
where the work to be indexed is important and the index is
severely limited for space, the preliminary reading must be
even more thorough than usual.

On the other hand, there are limits also to what even a very
generous publisher is prepared to pay for a short index, and
he is unlikely to be moved to pay for eighty hours' work on a
index of perhaps four octavo pages. Most indexers will readily
admit the necessity for some kind of compromise on this point,
and might well be prepared to consider payment based on
results—that is, on the amount of work produced. Nor is this
entirely unreasonable for, if an indexer knows in advance that
he is only required to produce a four-page index he will avoid
providing entries for one twice this size and may be able to
cut down on some of the other work which would be involved
in producing a large index. Assuming therefore that payment
is to be made by the number of pages of the actual published
index, how should the charge be calculated?

There are two possible systems. First, payment can be made
by fixing an arbitrary piece-work figure—say £2 per index
page—which would not work out very differently from the payment by hours spent system outlined above, the indexer of books

of general interest (and that would be the vast majority) benefiting at the expense of the technical indexer, though an adjustment could be made in the case of highly technical works. The second method is based on the author's total profits from his book. Take, for example, the sales of a small semi-technical work of some 250 pages, four of which are devoted to an index. If 5,000 copies of the book are sold at £2 each, the author's royalties might (allowing for lower percentages on overseas sales, etc.) amount to £500. Here the payment amounts to £2 per page, though—one hastens to add—there is no suggestion that this sum must inevitably come from the author's pocket! (Many publishers' agreements nowadays contain a clause to the effect that the author is expected to provide an adequate index as part of the MS.) Naturally it is impossible to hold up payment to the indexer until the majority of the sales have been made, and, as an indexer expects to be paid as soon as his work is completed, it will be reasonable to assume that sales of the book will be at least as large as the first issue of the first edition— in other words, the publisher confirms his faith in the book which he has already shown in ordering five thousand copies to be printed.

Without vaunting unduly the educational and professional accomplishments of indexers, it will perhaps be generally agreed that a good indexer has—in addition to his or her indexing skill—a general knowledge well above average. The specialist indexer, who is chosen to index a particular book because of his knowledge of the subject, very often possesses technical qualifications and at least some experience in a technical field. Not to belabour the point unduly, the indexer is therefore a skilled worker who should not be paid at purely clerical rates. And since he usually takes a professional pride and interest in his work the indexer deserves well of his employer. It is a wise precaution, where the publisher has mentioned no fee, for the indexer to quote an estimated fee for approval, before he commences work on the index.

At this point it may be acceptable to give one or two examples of current practice in the payment for indexing. Information on this aspect is extremely scanty, largely owing to the unorganised state of the indexing profession in Great Britain, and to the fact that much indexing is commissioned on a semi-

personal basis—that is to say, that the indexer is on friendly
terms with the publisher so that the reward is likely to be
calculated in some cases on an amicable rather than a scientific
basis. The two main systems which prevail at the present time,
however, appear to be based on opposite concepts. In the first
instance, indexers are paid at the rate of about ten pounds per
thousand page references: that is:

Chiropody, 127, 129

would count as two references, while:

Chiropody, 127–9

would count as three. It may well be asked who counts the
references? In general the publisher is apparently willing to
accept the indexer's word for the total number involved without
independent checking of a more than cursory kind.

The second system is based on the number of hours spent on
constructing the index, the payment being usually at the rate
of £0.50 per hour, though both publishers and indexers seem
now to be in agreement that this figure is too low, and that it
should be £0.75 or even £1 per hour. Again, the publisher
rarely challenges the indexer's estimate of the hours involved,
and as a result the indexer is inclined to undercharge in his
effort to avoid over-charging.

It will be seen that these two systems represent respectively
payment by results and payment by work done. That they have
worked so smoothly speaks well for the personal relationship
between indexers and publishers, but it may be questioned
whether these systems will continue to stand the test of modern
conditions. To illustrate the differing opinions on this point the
statements of two leading publishers may be apposite. One
publisher reports:

'We are hard put to it to find anyone reliable and competent [for indexing].'

while an equally well-known publisher writes:

'I should have supposed that any well-known firm of publishers would know quite well how and where to find indexers
who were reliable and competent; I can only say that,

F

speaking as the responsible editor of a very large firm of publishers, I find no difficulty in doing so. Agreed, they vary; but why not? Judging by the correspondence that comes my way, there are far more reliable indexers seeking indexes than indexes seeking indexers.'

It is also interesting to note that the second publishing house was established very much more recently than the first—somewhat of a paradox, since it might have been supposed that the older organisations would have built up a more solid reserve of indexers than the newer publishers could possibly do. Conversations with publishers will however reveal that indexers are recruited in the most individual and incalculable fashion, and that no distinguishable pattern of engaging such essential helpers emerges even after a lengthy survey. It may be added that some of the best publishing houses make certain of having good indexers always available by paying them an annual retainer.

It must be admitted that whatever system is used, the results are disappointing from the point of view of the indexer, who might earn many times the same amount in helping in a bar, mending television sets, or knitting pullovers. On the other hand, there are certain advantages: the work is ordered in advance at a fixed figure, the work can be carried out at home, no set hours are involved, and little equipment or work-space is needed. The task is often congenial and interesting, rush jobs may be paid at a higher figure and, as time goes on and the work of the indexer is recognised to be of a high standard, there may be as much more forthcoming as the indexer can reasonably manage to spare time to do. The trend is now towards more and more indexes and towards a higher standard of indexing; publishers who issue books without any kind of index or with inadequate indexes are very often slated in the more serious reviews, and many more libraries and private book-collectors are thus inclined to turn down a book which lacks an index. The prospects for indexers in the immediate future are therefore brighter than they have ever been, and so far the competition is not so keen that a good indexer need despair of work to do.

All the same, indexing is not a full-time career except for a very few people. It remains a spare-time, almost cottage-industry—or, rather, hobby—in which intelligent men and women can indulge their ability and knowledge to advantage. Like a good proof-reader, a good indexer can do much to improve a book, to make it more usable and to help the reader to a better understanding of its contents. The time has yet to come when the name of the indexer will as a matter of course be given at the head of the index, but it is to be hoped it is not too far ahead. A credit such as this would add to the authority of the index so that eventually the browser who sees the name of a well-known indexer at the head of the index in a book will recognise the volume as the product of a publisher who takes his job seriously.

Checking,
layout
and style

The value of any index lies in its service
for quick reference.
UNIVERSITY OF CHICAGO PRESS:
Manual of Style

IT IS POSSIBLE TO HAND OVER the index in the form of slips to the printer for setting-up in type. If this is done, the main points to watch are clarity, correct indentation and strict order. The latter can be achieved by pencilling in a running number on the top right-hand corner of each slip encircled to indicate that it is for the printer's convenience only and is not to be printed. There is no reason why a satisfactory index should not be printed from such material, and this was in fact the usual form of manuscript index in earlier days.

It is preferable, however, to have the index typed out double-spaced on quarto paper in the form in which it is to be printed, for this facilitates the setting-up of type. The printer finds slips slower and more difficult to handle—though some authors have overcome this objection to some extent by mounting the manuscript slips on quarto paper—whereas the presentation of an index in correct manuscript form means that it can be set up almost as quickly as the text of the book itself.

When the index is typed out the author should have clearly in mind its eventual form in print. A glance at a number of good printed indexes will help in doing so. Before typing is begun, the slips should be carefully edited, ambiguities and obscurities removed, and adjustments effected.

The adjustments include first of all ensuring that page references are in exact numerical order under each heading. If the index has been compiled in the order of the pages of the book this is fairly easy, but afterthoughts often cause additions to be made out of order. It is not necessary to rewrite the slips, if they have been clearly written: amendments can be made on the existing slips:

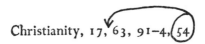

Christianity, 17, 63, 91–4, 54

Another adjustment which should be made is the correction of the alphabetical sub-arrangement of aspects, sub-headings, etc., after the main headings:

Engineering, 97–121
  electrical, 88
  structural, 101–12
  mechanical, 120–21

It is usual to insert a comma after the heading and before the first of the page-references. Further page-references are also separated by commas, but there is no need for any punctuation mark after the last page-reference. Where sub-headings follow on the same line, a colon should be inserted after the heading and before the first sub-heading. Semi-colons should separate the rest of the sub-headings from each other:

Engineering, 97–121
Engineering: electrical, 88; mechanical, 120–21;
  structural, 101–12

Successive sub-headings on separate lines beneath the heading should be indented three or five letters for clarity. Additional clarity can be secured by allowing a half-space between entries:

Milk
  boiled, 187, 355
  certified, 184–5

Molasses, 197

Mustard, 237

but the allowance of half-spaces between entries will reduce the number of possible entries, and is by no means essential. Where further indentation is necessary for sub-headings of sub-headings, another three spaces should be allowed:

Milk
certified, 184–5
bottled, 184
in bulk, 185
clean, 153, 157, 185
Molasses, 197

Footnotes can be indicated by n (or nn where more than one footnote refers):

deceit, 37n, 128nn

Volume numbers should also be shown, a semi-colon indicating the break with the next volume:

falsehood, I 23, 46; II 78–82, 143

Many indexes in former days, and even some recent indexes, have been printed in several sequences. In the field of topography, for instance, many of the older books used to give one index of places, another of people, and sometimes a third of general subjects. In some books concerned with foreign countries and languages—especially those using non-Roman alphabets—separate indexes were made for such items as foreign words and phrases, and subject indexes were often made separate from proper names. There is no need for this. If it is desired to indicate clearly the distinction between various types of entry, it is possible to do so in the same sequence by the intelligent use of typography. For example, a book on Italy may have many references to famous places, to people, and to other books, and in addition to many Italian phrases. These can all be combined in one alphabetical sequence, with the subjects covered in such a manner as the following, without the use of any but the various sorts of type in the stock of every good printer:

Lasciate ogni speranza voi ch'entrate, 72
Lenten customs, 83–6
Lire, 2–3
Livorno, 123–7
Loring, Francis, 197
Lucca, 203–17
'Lucia di Lammermoor', 52

As this is set out, there is little doubt concerning the purport of each item, and a note at the beginning of the index will explain the meaning of the different sorts used:

INDEX

Entries in SMALL CAPITALS denote places. Those in *italics* are for phrases in Italian. Books, operas, etc., are printed within inverted commas

When typing the index there is no need to imitate the typesetting: a few simple manuscript indications will be sufficient:

ital.   Lasciate ogni speranza voi ch'entrate, 72

Lenten customs, 83–6

Lire, 2–3

S.C.   Livorno, 123–7

Loring, Francis, 197

S.C.   Lucca, 203–17

'Lucia di Lammermoor', 52

Any good printer can achieve such distinctions as these and many more difficult: certainly there is no need for separate sequences which would only delay and sometimes prevent the reader's quick reference to the text. It will be noticed that the distinctions above have been achieved without the use of bold type. Italics should always be used either for quoted phrases in foreign languages or for the quoted titles of books—unless this form has already been used for some other purpose—but not for the names of authors:

Dickens, Charles, *David Copperfield*, 193

An interesting example of these principles applied to a non-European language is given in the magnificent 150-page combined Index and Glossary of Arabic Words in Charles M. Doughty's *Travels in Arabia Deserta* (Jonathan Cape and the Medici Society, 1888, and various subsequent editions), from which the following abbreviated extract is taken:

Power of the Air, 450

Ppahppah! voice of a dumb Arabian, II. 8

Praevaesa, town in Albania, II. 507

Prisoners in war, *v. Jehâd*

Pro Deo et Patria (for God and the Fatherland), motto read on a Bedouin's cutlass, 457

Ptolemy, the geographer, 94, 617

Pulse: they think an hakîm should know all a sick man's state in only handling his ——, 256; II, 55, 356

With regard to the last entry, the stroke could have been replaced by 'p': wherever a word repeats the heading, this form of abbreviation will be found generally acceptable.

Where references are made to paragraphs and not to pages, this fact should clearly be indicated at the foot of *every* page of the index in bold-face type:

bf   References are to paragraph numbers

Although alphabetical order is necessary for the index as a whole, and for the order of most sub-headings, there are cases where other arrangements are preferable. For instance, in biographical and historical works, entries under the names of persons can very often be arranged chronologically according to events in the man's life with advantage:

> Fitzgerald, Arthur: birth, 2; education, 4–7; university career, 19–22; appointed curate, 24; etc. etc.

the advantages of such an arrangement are obvious. Similarly, a chronological arrangement under such items as the names of cities and states is often of the greatest use. In some scientific works it may also be necessary to sacrifice alphabetic arrangement of sub-headings to a more orderly arrangement by the classification of species, by numerical order of chemical compounds, etc.

Variations in the form of name can be economically shown by using oblique strokes:

> Bartholin/Bartholinus/Berthelsen, Kaspar (1585–1629), 17–21

The alphabetisation of the index must be carefully considered: there are two main methods. The first is known as the 'all through' method, which involves the arrangement of all entries in a strict alphabetical arrangement, letter by letter, no matter how many words are involved. The second arrangement is word by word, in which all the entries beginning with one word are arranged before those beginning with a second word are handled. The difference in effect can be considerable as will be seen from the following example:

'All through'	*'Word by Word'*
East Anglia	East Anglia
Eastbourne	East End
East End	East Grinstead
Easter Day	East Ham
Eastern time	East Indies
East Grinstead	East Malling
East Ham	Eastbourne
East Indies	Easter Day
East Malling	Eastern time

In this example, exactly the same words are included in each column, yet the second word in the left-hand column becomes the seventh in the right-hand column, while the last word in the right-hand is the fifth in the left-hand sequence. It can therefore be understood how great are the chances of a reader missing an item when he is dealing with several books, some of which use the 'all through' and some the 'word by word' method. The difference is all the greater, the lengthier the index, and will be more apparent in indexes consisting mainly of entries containing more than one word. In any case, there will be some difference whatever the length of the index or the composition of individual entries. Both varieties of index are, moreover, so general and well-established that there is little point in arguing their respecting advantages and defects, for each has a large body of opinion behind it.

The author should therefore determine which is the more suitable from his own particular point of view, and should then ensure that the system is applied consistently throughout, for a combination of the two methods would prove disastrous. It may be of help to mention what systems are in use by some of the most famous standard works:

'All through'	*'Word by Word'*
Statesman's Year-Book	Whitaker's Almanack
Chambers's Encyclopaedia	Kelly's Post Office London
Encyclopaedia Britannica	Directory
The Blue Guides	H. W. Wilson's Periodical
Encyclopedia of Zionism	indexes
and Israel	Library Association's Sub-
	ject Index to Periodicals

From these lists it will be seen that the field is fairly equally divided, and that there is no present possibility of one system becoming general. Nor do these two systems exhaust the different methods of arrangement possible, for a glance at the telephone directory will show that the nation has subconsciously accustomed itself to still another variety, in which minor variations are ignored in favour of an alphabetical arrangement by significant word only. The following abbreviated extract from the London telephone directory will demonstrate the method employed:

> Watson, William
> Watson, Winifred
> Watson, W. and Sons, Ltd.
> Watson, W. T.
> Watson, Wylie
> Watson's British Drawing Ink Co., Ltd.
> Watson-Baker Co. Ltd.
> Watson Smyth, Mrs. M. M.
> Watsonian Club (London)
> Watson's, Printers
> Watsons (Floor Coverings) Ltd.

This is a variation of the 'word by word' system, in which adaptations have been made to fit it to one of the most complicated indexes in the world. In the third entry the word 'and' has been ignored, and 'Sons' takes its alphabetical place before 'T'. In the sixth entry the apostrophe 's' is ignored. In the tenth, (Printers) is ignored. A careful study of the directory will reveal many more ingenious and sensible adjustments which are justified by the fact that the index is comparatively simple to use in spite of its vast size. The Post Office would do a service to indexers in publishing the rules on which the arrangement of entries in their directories is based. There are however two very good explanations of the methods of arrangement of similar complicated large-scale indexes in the preliminary pages of the index volumes of the *Encyclopaedia Britannica* and *Chambers's Encyclopaedia*, which can be read with profit both by users of these encyclopaedias and by those intending to compile indexes of their own.

Page references should be carefully stated. For instance, the following two references are by no means equal:

$$52, 53, 54 \quad \neq \quad 52\text{--}4$$

in the left-hand example the inference is that the subject referred to is mentioned intermittently on pages 52, 53, and 54. The right-hand example implies that the whole or a considerable portion of these pages is devoted to a connected treatment of the subject. This is a helpful and necessary distinction and should be observed at all times, even though abbreviation could be achieved by running the page references together.

There is also a definite style in giving page references which should be followed consistently. References to a sequence of pages should only repeat the tens or hundreds digits when there is any possibility of ambiguity:

	90–91	*not*	90–1
	121–6	*not*	121–26
but	13–17	*not*	13–7
and	97–101	*not*	97–1 *or* 97–01
	125–31	*not*	125–131

When the index has been completed it should be carefully checked to ensure that no necessary references have been omitted. In doing so it is wise to consult a dictionary of synonyms and antonyms once again, or even to consult a list of subject-headings such as is used by cataloguers in libraries for compiling subject-catalogues. Suitable works of this nature are described in Part Three.

The index slips should then be checked with the book. To do this, the slips should be resorted in page number order by the first page-reference on each slip:

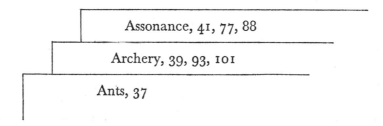

Assonance, 41, 77, 88

Archery, 39, 93, 101

Ants, 37

As each slip is checked with the relevant page, it is either laid aside if there are no other page-references on it, or resorted into the next page position according to the next page-reference. Thus, after the reference to Assonance on page 41 has been checked, the slip for Assonance would be moved forward to page 77, and would be checked with that page when the indexer again meets with that slip. Although this would appear a laborious process, it is in fact remarkably speedy and accurate, and it is straightforward because it only involves going straight through the book page by page. Any other method would involve unnecessary turning up of particular page references, waste of time, and some possibility of omitting to check individual page-references. If the indexer can obtain the assistance of a friend in making this check, the work can be carried out at great speed and with very little hardship to either.

The slips are then resorted into alphabetical order ready for typing. When the typing is completed the entries on the slips are carefully checked with the typescript. To do this it is essential for two people to undertake the task, one reading and the other checking. If only one person does the whole of the checking, there is great danger of errors creeping in which will be very difficult to discover later on.

In the typescript it may be necessary to carry forward parts of entries to the next page in some cases: this should be done with a clear indication of continuation:

Art, German [contd]
    nineteenth-century, 83–9, 97
    contemporary, 101–14
    present-day trends, 126–32

This is also another example of the substitution of chronological arrangement for alphabetical, to meet the needs of students who wish to follow the development of a subject.

Where the index has been constructed and prepared by someone other than the author, checking is all the more necessary. If possible, the original slips should be secured in addition to the script, since a page-by-page check can then be carried out by the author in a similar fashion to that described above. Otherwise, sample entries should be selected and scrutinised for accuracy of description, page-references, etc. The whole index should also be read through by the author in order to ensure that it is adequate and that no important ideas have been omitted. Discrepancies of description, subordination, etc., will often be immediately apparent.

When the author is satisfied that the index is adequate for the purpose, it can then be despatched to the publisher, but proofs should again be carefully examined and corrected, since errors may still creep in, and may include transposition of entries. wrong page-references, misspellings, omissions, wrong indentations, etc. A careful watch should be kept for the necessity for including continuation headings at the top of columns or pages (as above) wherever these have been omitted by the printer. A specimen page of an index, with proof-corrections and their interpretation, is given in Part Three. Throughout the work of index making and printing, the main requirement is consistency, without which clarity and ease of reference are forfeited.

Collaboration
with the
printer

*I have just made a dozen tests. Five of the
references in the text which I looked up in
the index found no place in it at all. Four
more were virtually unidentifiable: for what
is the use of seventeen undifferentiated
references after a famous name?*

ALEC CLIFTON-TAYLOR: An Open
Letter to a Publisher

IT HAS ALREADY BEEN SUGGESTED that the author should first
ascertain from the publisher how much space has been allotted
to the index, before actually embarking on its construction.
This will save the time and temper of all three participants in
its making and production: author, publisher and printer. In
calculating the number of pages, allowance should be made for
any title, explanation and indentation on the first page of the
index. Allowance should also be made for spaces between every
pair of letters after the first: a space equivalent to three lines
will be sufficient, since there is no need to head each section
with the relevant letter. In constructing the index it is well to
make entries for only 98 per cent of the possible number of
entries: this will allow for any last-minute insertions, and for
those instances where the publisher and the printer may also
have suggestions to make for improvement which may occupy
some little space.

To underestimate in this way is wise, since any cutting down
of entries inevitably leads to difficulties. As has been implied, a
good index is a complete work in itself, each entry being linked
with its fellows in a system somewhat resembling a spider's web,
and the elision of one entry may upset the references to several
others.

Nevertheless, since revision of this kind may sometimes be

necessary, it is a good policy to enter 'tracings' of any references made on the main slip:

Ants, 25–8
see also ref: Insects
see ref: Formicidae

The 'tracings' here are of two kinds: the first states that under the heading Insects is a reference 'see also Ants', while from Formicidae there is a single reference 'see Ants'. Notes of this kind are invaluable when there is any possibility of omissions having to be made later.

In the case of books likely to go into second or further editions, these 'tracings' have still further uses. Whenever there is a possibility of future revised editions the original entry slips should be kept carefully. When the second edition is being prepared, all passages which have been corrected, altered, re-written, omitted or added, should be marked at the time. On completion of the revision of the book, the original slips should be resorted into page number order, compared with the marked passages, and the necessary corrections, deletions and new additions made. The 'tracing' here are of the greatest importance, since the elision of an entry involves consideration whether any of the 'see' or 'see also' references is rendered useless, or whether it should be omitted or altered. Additions to the slips may also involve an extension of the original 'see also' slips to include the new subjects, and also perhaps the making of 'see' references to include new synonyms. Before the index is typed, the slips should then be read through once again to make certain that any references occasioned by the addition of new entries have been made. Even when the new index has been typed, it should be read through carefully from the point of view of the reader, for the old saying about 'new wine in old bottles' applies as much to amended indexes as to any other subject.

Instructions to the printer concerning the use of bold type, italics, indentation, etc., should be clear and in the form indicated in the example given in Part III. It is essential to have at least one proof of an index, and, if possible, two. When the first proof arrives it is well to check it thoroughly with a friend who is prepared to read the original typescript. Spelling mistakes, punctuation, indentation, broken letters, wrong page-references, and any other errors should be carefully and clearly corrected. The British Standard on Proof-Correction (B.S. 1219: 1958) gives many useful tips on this work, and recommends that each page should be initialled and dated before return to the printer.

If no further proof is demanded, errors may still creep in. The two most usual causes are:

(1) lines may have become transposed when being corrected. This of course applies to all printing, and most usually occurs in newspapers.

(2) new errors may occur as lines in which there are corrections to be made are recomposed.

Unless the printer and his reader are therefore of the first rank, a second set of proofs is advisable.

In constructing an index the author will have built up a workmanlike set of subject-headings. If he is likely to write several books on the same or related subjects, the possibility of maintaining a permanent standard list of subject-headings should be considered. This involves some extra and rather tedious work at the beginning, but will save much time and duplication of effort in the long run. The subject-headings list should consist of one slip for each subject-heading, with the references clearly marked as indicated in the following examples:

Fruit
　　see also individual varieties: Apples, Pears;
　　Blackberries, etc.

Apples
　　see also ref. from: Fruit

Zambia
see ref. from: Rhodesia, Northern; Northern
Rhodesia

Rhodesia, Northern
see Zambia

Northern Rhodesia
see Zambia

This type of subject-headings list will remind the author of all the related headings for which he must make references. Naturally, in constructing a new index there will be new headings to be used (entries for which he should add to his basic list), but this will prove a good foundation for his work, and will become increasingly valuable as time goes on. It will also act as a check-list for ensuring that no important subject is missed in his later books.

On this point, the value of published book classifications is of great importance. Book classifications are systems of arranging books by symbols in such a way that the books on related subjects are brought close together, and notes in the classification indicate other related subjects in other parts of the classification. In this way, book classifications not only provide logical positions on the shelves for subjects on which books have been written, but they also indicate those items of knowledge on which little or nothing has so far been published. In constructing a book, it is worth while checking one of the standard systems of book classification—such as the Dewey Decimal system, or the Bliss or Library of Congress classification systems—to ensure that no important aspects have been overlooked. Copies of these classifications are readily available in most medium and large libraries, and a perusal of their schedules invariably brings new ideas to light with benefit to both author and reader.

G

Part two

Wider indexing

Different types
of material
and their
indexing

The indexing of complex and involved subjects requires a thorough knowledge of the subject matter.

UNIVERSITY OF CHICAGO PRESS:
Manual of Style

MANY PEOPLE NEED INDEXES for material quite different from books. In the ordinary affairs of everyday life everything needs to be sorted and indexed carefully if the most is to be made of it, and if time is to be saved. Most people do not keep indexes of this nature, because some effort is required and it is necessary to devote a certain amount of time to the task at regular intervals. This is unfortunate, since such an omission very often causes loss of business and profit, and deprives the man-in-the-street of that sense of control over his private affairs which such indexes can give. In hobbies and in pastimes, the construction of an index can secure greater enjoyment from the collection of material, be it discs and tapes or butterflies, and may sometimes reveal new and unsuspected aspects of the subject.

One of the most usual forms of material which requires indexing is private correspondence. However correspondence is arranged it will fail to reveal its full resources by itself. The construction of an index is the only method of getting full value from correspondence files. The two main features of correspondence are its subjects and the names of the correspondents. From the point of view of the continuity of correspondence and the ensuring of answers being made promptly, it is essential to arrange most correspondence files alphabetically by the names of the correspondents, and to sub-arrange the letters chronologically, with the latest letters to the fore. This arrangement automatically provides its own index of correspondents. To this should be added a subject index. A circular letter is for example

sent to various correspondents enquiring about bird songs heard
on a certain date. The subject index entries for this would read:

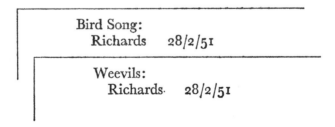

Bird Song:
     Richards   28/2/51   6/8/51
     Appleby   3/3/51
     Anderson   5/3/51

Thrush:
     Richards 28/2/51
     Appleby   3/3/51

Robin:
     Richards   6/8/51
     Anderson   5/3/51

by which the indexer is able to look up all his correspondence
on bird songs in general, or turn straight away to those letters
which refer to one particular species of bird, and at the same
time all the correspondence with Richards, Appleby, Anderson,
etc., is kept together under the individual correspondents'
names. This is especially important where two or more subjects
are mentioned in the same letter:

Bird Song:
     Richards   28/2/51

Weevils:
     Richards.   28/2/51

for by such a system the full subject-contents of each letter are
revealed. Ease of reference can further be ensured by underlining relevant passages in the correspondence and writing a
key-word in the margin. A simple index of this kind will require
very little time each week to keep it completely up to date.

     The example just given relates to nature study, but the

principles can be applied to most subjects without very much modification. Correspondence discussing the details of postage stamps, the growing of roses, the developments in radio, and a hundred and one other subjects, can be dealt with just as satisfactorily by arranging the letters themselves alphabetically by correspondents, and by making a detailed subject-index to their contents.

The arrangement and indexing of correspondence for business purposes from the business office point of view is discussed later in this book, and is moreover well covered by a number of excellent standard works on the subject, which are mentioned in the chapter on Further Reading.

Most people have collections of photographs of their own, some of their own family and of friends, and others of buildings and scenes in this and foreign countries. When showing them to friends, however, they very often find it difficult to discover a particular photograph quickly. One way of overcoming this is to write a contents list on a page at the beginning of each album. This is a rather cumbrous method, and is not at all satisfactory once the collection starts growing beyond two or three albums. A better method is to give each photograph a running number as it is added to the collection. In this way unmounted photographs, and those of very different sizes can be dealt with immediately as well as those in the albums. The index can then be constructed with great ease and informality:

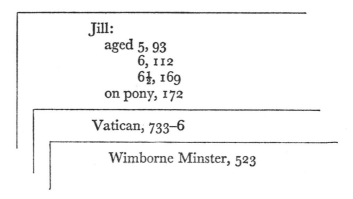

Jill:
   aged 5, 93
      6, 112
      6½, 169
  on pony, 172

Vatican, 733–6

Wimborne Minster, 523

and the references to people and places can all be kept within the same alphabetical sequence. The same system can also be made to exploit all the details of the photographs in a way that the arrangement of the photographs themselves—however skilful—could not possibly do. If, for instance, a photograph of 'Jill, aged 10', also shows an excellent view of Eros in the background, the point can be brought out fully in the index, even if the photograph itself has been put with all the others of Jill:

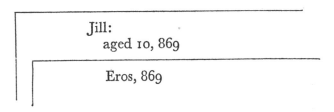

Jill:
    aged 10, 869

Eros, 869

Further applications will suggest themselves to readers as they consider their own particular needs and interests. For example, the photographer who makes a hobby of recording different types of signposts may want to classify them in several different ways: perhaps by countries, by types, by lettering, etc. However he arranges his collection, the remaining aspects can be shown by means of an index of this type.

Personal indexes of this kind, which are not likely to extend to unmanageable proportions, are best kept on slips in loose-leaf holders which can be handled in much the same way as a book, and are easily portable from place to place, since the slips are kept in position and in order by metal staples. Shops specialising in office equipment can supply 'sheaf-holders' and suitably-sized slips of this kind readily at a moderate price.

The habit of keeping scrap-books of interesting material is happily not yet past. One man will clip and mount amusing or poignant passages from speeches, or copy out passages from books he has read. Another will mount photographs, cuttings, etc., from local newspapers, leaflets, and other ephemeral publications, for the purpose of recording the life and changes of the community. A third will collect greetings-cards, decorations, and other scraps. To all of these an index is essential unless they are content to treat their collection as an unorganised mass of trivia, or are gifted with superhuman memories. Even if they are, those who inherit such material will find an index invaluable. Any index of this type of material should consist of brief entries and can be kept in an informal fashion. It is well, how-ever, to maintain it on slips until the commonplace- or scrap-book is full, and then to type it out and mount it in the front, immediately following the title-page. Where there are not too many items on each page, a page-reference will be sufficient; otherwise, each item should be separately numbered to facilitate speed of reference. From the nineteenth century many scrap- and commonplace-books have survived, and there is no doubt that the libraries which have inherited them would have made much more use of them if they had been properly indexed in this fashion.

Collections of objects of art, scientific specimens, or other material, sometimes reach large proportions. An index can add much to their enjoyment and exploitation. It is here that the form of the index should be very carefully considered before embarking on its construction. A collection of specimens of butterflies and moths, for instance, should be arranged by genera, species, etc., but even so an alphabetical index may not necessarily be the first adjunct. If the collection is large and complicated, it may be necessary to arrange the index by one of the standard recognised systems of classification, and to supply an alphabetical index to this. In other words, the main index becomes a guide or catalogue to the specimens in the order in which they are displayed in their cases, and the supplementary alphabetical index is only used when it is required to refer quickly to a specimen whose genus or species is not immediately remembered.

Objects of art—statuettes, paintings, drawings, illustrations in books and catalogues, coins and medals, bric-a-brac, etc.—may be scattered in many rooms throughout a house. Where the collection has been built up on a definite plan, the index may be required to reveal all the examples of any given school, period or country, and it should therefore be considered whether the alphabetical system is best, or whether it is not preferable to make a classified index of schools, periods, countries, etc., with an alphabetical index of artists, sculptors, painters, engravers, forms, movements, etc. In doing so it is well to consult the cata-logues to such galleries as the Wallace Collection, the Barber Institute of Fine Art, etc., which give much guidance on good methods of catalogue and index arrangement in this field.

During the past hundred years or so, much progress has been made in transcribing local records, which reveal the history of the community in the past. Chief among these has been the invaluable system of transcribing parish registers and similar material in the archives of churches, towns and villages. In these apparently dull records can be found important details of ancestors, local events, the impact of national events on local affairs, and even details which contribute considerably to the national history itself. Transcription itself is not sufficient, although many registers in the past have been reproduced without a key to their contents. An index is essential if the register is to be used to the full. People, places and events should all be indexed, and the utmost care should be taken to distinguish between like names and events in different periods. The same names occur again and again over the course of centuries, and some such form as the following should be adopted to differentiate between them:

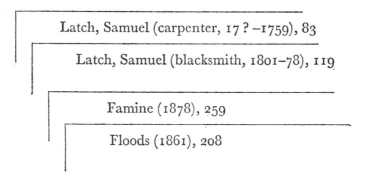

Latch, Samuel (carpenter, 17 ? –1759), 83

Latch, Samuel (blacksmith, 1801–78), 119

Famine (1878), 259

Floods (1861), 208

The addition of explanatory phrases in brackets after the entry will help the reader to identify the item he requires quickly, and will break up a long series of references under the same heading. Such work is arduous, but those who follow bless the (often unnamed) indexer who has helped them in their research.

In business affairs, one of the most difficult items to trace is the average little-known trade name. Another even less easy to trace is the trade-mark. Both of these can be indexed briefly and fairly easily together with any mottoes which may be used by the firms concerned. Since it is not done nationally except in a very haphazard fashion, much trade is lost through inability to trace such items quickly. Trade names are comparatively straightforward, as long as care is taken to index any possible alternative forms under which they may be sought:

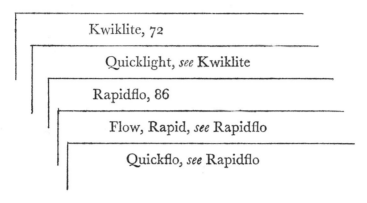

Kwiklite, 72

Quicklight, *see* Kwiklite

Rapidflo, 86

Flow, Rapid, *see* Rapidflo

Quickflo, *see* Rapidflo

References in these examples are given to numbers, it being assumed that they refer to a collection of trade catalogues kept in a numerical arrangement; but the index can be made complete in itself by making an index of manufacturers and their trade-marks and names, in the following fashion:

Kwiklite.
Blue Match Co., Ltd., Broome End, Coventry.

Blue Match Co., Ltd., Broome End, Coventry.
Trade name: Kwiklite
Trade-mark: Blue match, with red flame

Trade-marks are not as easy to index, since they are symbols, and not words. The best method is to analyse all distinguishable features of any trade-mark, including any names or parts of names which may be incorporated in the design (which are sometimes transpositions of the real name of the firm). For example, if the manufacturer of a shoe polish uses as a trade-mark a symbol showing the sun reflected in a polished shoe, the index entries could be made in the following fashion:

> Sun (reflected in shoe)
> Evabrite Manufacturing Co.,
> Northampton
>
> Shoe (showing reflection of sun)
> Evabrite Manufacturing Co.,
> Northampton

Naturally, many trade-marks are not so easy to index, but as all of them are designed to be memorable, the first essential is to consider what they immediately call to mind and to index under the nearest word-equivalent.

Mottoes can be treated in a similar way. If the motto of the shoe polish firm is REFLECT ON THE SHINE, index entries can be made under both the first and the last words, and for any similar words by which the motto might be imperfectly recalled at different times. Even when the index does not reveal the desired information straight away, it is easier to glance quickly through a number of slips or cards, than to page through the voluminous catalogues and advertisement pages which might or might not contain it.

Concordances exist for the works of the very great authors. Nevertheless, the works of many writers, either because they are too obscure or because they are too recent, lack any index to their contents. The work of compiling a concordance is laborious and monumental, but if a good example is used, such as Bartlett's Concordance to the works of Shakespeare, or Strong's Concordance to the Bible, it is possible to construct and publish a most useful concordance which will be of great use to oneself and to others interested in the same author. The main essential is to index all the significant words by which any particular phrase might be remembered, and to give sufficient details of the passage to distinguish it from any similar passages. In doing so, unsuspected details of the development of a writer's work, and similarities hitherto unperceived between one work and another may be discovered, and thus a real contribution to literary research may be made. Such indexing may also show unknown links with the works of other writers, and give new impetus to investigation abandoned for lack of evidence.

Indexes of this nature have other uses as well. It is not usually possible or desirable to send one's collection to friends or fellow-workers in distant cities or in far-off countries, but one can at least send them a copy of the index which will afford some idea of the scope and nature of the collection. If the index is in typescript or manuscript it can be reproduced for a small sum, and copies thus become easily available for those interested in the same subjects. The exchange of indexes in this way may well stimulate the exchange of duplicates, the acquisition of new items, and the discovery of unsuspected deficiencies and treasures. It will certainly add to the store of knowledge on the subject.

In this connection, the impact of computers on the making of concordances is of great interest. Readers may care to examine Stephen Maxfield Parrish's concordances to Matthew Arnold and W. B. Yeats (Cornell University Press, 1959 and 1963 respectively) which are excellent examples of the new technique. Briefly, the process comprises punching the lines of verse on IBM cards, and adding page and line numbers. Lines too long for a single card are continued on extra cards; and variant lines are also added. The cards for each poem are precoded by an abbreviated title-card, but full titles are also indexed. The material is then transferred to magnetic tape. The IBM 704 machine then proceeds to search the tape and index all but common words (e.g. a, an, by, the, to, etc.), together with the identifying page number, abbreviated title, and line number. A useful by-product is a frequency list of the use of individual words, from which style can be more closely studied.

The indexing of music and recordings

A really good index will in most cases itself give the information wanted.

STEPHEN LEACOCK

THERE ARE THREE TYPES of material which last longer and keep in better condition the less they are handled: these are music, recordings and films. No proud owner of music can view without dismay the visitor who carelessly leafs through sheet after sheet of songs or piano solos in search of one particular piece. The damage which can be done in one or two hasty searches of this kind is however negligible compared with what can be done to a collection of recordings if they are often turned over in large numbers at great speed. The trouble is that every item must be examined individually, and this involves much handling. Whereas it is quite simple to glance along a row of books and read their titles without actually touching each one of them, this is an impossible method in the case of most music and records. They rarely have spines on which titles can be lettered, and they are very much more fragile. What, then, can be done to reduce the risk of damage, and yet to ensure that any item can be found immediately?

The answer is, to construct an index of them. This need not necessarily be an elaborate affair, and it can certainly be informal and kept with a minimum of effort, and yet save everyone much time and lengthen the life of the music and recordings. It has other advantages, too: if the index is kept in convenient form, such as on loose-leaf sheets or slips in a holder or binder, or on cards in a small filing-box, it can readily be consulted when looking through catalogues, or making out wants lists, and may prevent duplicates being bought. Copies can easily be prepared and sent to friends or other collectors, and the addition of various details will turn it into a valuable work of reference.

The main index entry for each item will naturally be made under the composer's name, and here a consideration arises which is not so prominent in the indexing of ordinary books: this is the factor of language and the spelling of names. Much important music is foreign in origin and the spelling of the names of composers is by no means standardised yet. So it is possible to find one record whose label gives the spelling TCHAIKOVSKY, while another may read TSCHAIKOWSKI. Other similar variations immediately spring to mind: GLAZUNOV and GLAZOUNOW, STRAVINSKY and STRAWINSKI. Some of the variants arise from the fact that the recordings have been made in different countries, for France—for instance—uses a different method for spelling out the names of eastern composers. In addition, there are such cases as composers who used two names —Peter Warlock and Philip Heseltine, for example—which have to be considered in making a satisfactory index.

To ensure that different forms of the same name are not used at different times in the same index, and to avoid duplication of purchases, it is a very good idea to use a standard encyclopaedia of music as a guide to the correct spelling to adopt. There are several useful volumes of this type on the market, any one of which would be helpful, and the form of name given in the volume should be strictly adhered to. There is the additional advantage that from the same reference work details of dates, brief outlines of lives and compositions, and much other valuable information can be gained. One of the most comprehensive works of this kind is Sir George Grove's *Dictionary of Music and Musicians* (10 volumes, Macmillan 1954; Supplement 1961), which contains detailed biographies and lists of compositions, and is fairly generally available. It is especially useful for British musicians. A very handy one-volume encyclopaedia is Thompson's *International Cyclopaedia of Music and Musicians* (Dent, 1964), which gives extensive treatment to the more important composers, and is especially useful for modern and less-known musicians. A less expensive work is Blom's *Everyman's Dictionary of Music* (5th edition, Dent, 1971), which gives sufficient basic information for the average index.

Gramophone record collectors have two works which are especially relevant: the American *Guide to long-playing records*, three volumes (New York, Knopf, 1955), which is arranged alphabetically by composer, sub-arranged by title, except that certain well-defined forms—such as concertos, masses, songs, motets, symphonies, etc—are grouped together and listed numerically by opus, edition, or date, or alphabetically by text or key. Dates of birth and death, and brief biographical details are given wherever possible, and there is an appendix of details of collections of societies, etc., and an index of performers. A similar British index is Francis F. Clough's and Geoffrey J. Cuming's *The World's Encyclopaedia of Recorded Music* (Sidgwick and Jackson, 1952) and its supplements.

Such works as these are invaluable guides, and will often prompt the indexer to make references and added entries which he would otherwise miss. Indeed, for small collections, the indexer may very well decide to dispense with an index of his own, and to use one of these reference works as his index instead, marking those items which he possesses, and entering in the margins those recordings for which there is no entry. But for any extensive collection, it will be necessary to make an index of one's own.

Although the entry under the composer is always the main entry, most collectors will require entries under other items as well. The chief points of interest for which extra entries may be needed are titles (especially where there are variations of titles, or where the title is known in several languages, or where there is a popular title—such as the Moonlight Sonata—which is unofficial); the artist or artists (especially where the performer is well known, or where he is playing an unusual rôle, such as a violinist playing the viola, etc.); the conductor; the solo instrument, in the case of concertos; the name of the orchestra or choir; the form of music—symphonies, concertos, etc.; and nationality, or period, where the collector is particularly interested in the music of individual countries or centuries.

It is unlikely that many collectors will require entries under all of these aspects, but most will need some of them. The construction of these entries is similar to that for book index entries. In the case of a record of Gigli singing 'Thy tiny hand is frozen', the entries would be:

Composer	Puccini:
	    La Bôhéme: Thy tiny hand is frozen
	        (Gigli)

Title	Bôhéme, La by Puccini

Title	Thy tiny hand is frozen
	    Puccini: La Bôhéme
	    Gigli

Artist	Gigli:
	    Thy tiny hand is frozen
	        (Bôhéme)

and additional entries, in similar fashion, could be made for the conductor and the orchestra.

A record of Cortot playing the Chopin First Piano Concerto, with the Boston Philharmonic Orchestra, conducted by Leopold Stokowski, would be entered:

Composer	Chopin:
	    First Piano Concerto (Cortot, and Boston
	        Philharmonic)

Artist	Cortot:
	    Chopin: First Piano Concerto (Boston
	        Philharmonic)

Orchestra	Boston Philharmonic Orchestra (Stokowski) Chopin: First Piano Concerto (Cortot)
Conductor	Stokowski: *see* Boston Philharmonic Orchestra

Form	Concertos:
	    Chopin: First Piano (Cortot and Boston
	        Philharmonic)

H

With these five forms of entry, most of the interests of listeners and collectors are covered, whether they are interested in composers, artists, orchestras, conductors, or concertos.

An index of entries such as these (with the addition of suitable finding numbers or symbols) is complete in itself. Serious collectors, however, may require rather more detailed information, and there is much which can be added and which will turn the index into a valuable and informative catalogue. Useful items of information which can be included are:

(*a*) the dates of birth and death, and the nationality of composers, artists, conductors, etc.

(*b*) a translation of any foreign title

(*c*) the number of sides of the records

(*d*) the time of playing, in minutes (very useful for planning concerts, etc.)

(*e*) the type of recording (such as long-playing, pre-electric, etc.)

(*f*) the maker of the record (especially for foreign recordings)

If many details are to be added, it is a good policy to use a larger form of index slip—say, 7 in. by 4 in., or 8 in. by 5 in., and this in its turn brings the possibility of economising in time by making several basic entries at once by using carbons. The carbon copies can be made with a typewriter or with a ball-pointed pen, and in this way four or five copies can be made at one time. The method is to make the main entry (i.e. the composer entry), and then to add to the additional copies the headings for the added entries—artists, title, orchestra, form, etc.—which can be typed or written in at the head of the carbon copies, if sufficient space is allowed for this purpose. By this method, all the information which is contained in the main entry is also on the added entries, which saves much turning from entry to entry in search of additional information, and reduces checking of details, since only the top slip need be checked for accuracy.

One of the most interesting developments of the post-war years has been the indexing of musical themes. The development is astounding in its possibilities: the method is so clever and yet so simple that it is surprising that it has remained for the twentieth century to discover it. The book which brought this method of identifying music within popular reach is Barlow and Morgenstern's *Dictionary of Musical Themes* (8th imp., Benn, 1967),[1] an American work with an international scope and appeal. Music is after all an international language, and the method explained in this book could be used in any country. Briefly, the system is based on the scale in C. The theme which it is desired to identify is first reduced to the key in C. Its notes are then read off—for example:

$$\Lambda \quad B \quad E \quad F\sharp \quad G$$

This notation is then found in the index which is arranged alphabetically, and against the entry for it is given a number referring to the theme which is given in musical notation in the body of the book. Naturally only the basic themes are given in this book, but by planning his indexing on the system explained, any collector could build up an index of themes to suit his own individual requirements. The same authors have also published a companion volume: *A Dictionary of Vocal Themes* (Benn, 1956).[2]

[1,2] Published in USA by Cronn Publishers

The
indexing
of films

IN THE UNITED STATES the film is rapidly becoming as much part of everyday life as the tape recorder and the television receiver. The number of projectors in private possession is such that many public libraries maintain film libraries as part of their ordinary service, and many people make their own films for various purposes. In Great Britain, the private use of film is not yet so general, but even so many enthusiasts are building up their own collections of films, and the application of a few simple rules of indexing at the start will both provide a key to the films and help to protect them from unnecessary handling and exhibition.

One of the most usual types of film in the home is that which records the life of the various members of the family, and more especially their holidays and travels. It is this kind of film which is especially worth indexing: the scenes very often have no connection with each other, and while it may be easy to identify people and places a few months after, what was so vivid at the time sooner or later fades into uncertainty. Moreover, when the collection of films has grown to more than ten or twelve, it is useful to be able to produce straight away the particular scene in mind, rather than run through several films and perhaps still miss it.

The indexing of films is very much like that of photographs, but the physical nature of the film requires rather more detailed treatment. The first step should be to list each film as it is added to the collection either by a suitable title, or by a running number. The number in the list should be repeated on the film itself and on its container, so that it can be identified immediately. In the list it is helpful to include the dates covered by the

116

film, and to leave a column for any remarks which may be necessary:

No.	Title	Dates	Remarks
14	Falmouth Holiday	10–24 Aug. '52	colour. 10m.
15	School Play	6 Dec. '52	5m.

The time of running has been included in the remarks column, but where several people may be likely to use the films at different times it is advisable to give this item a separate column, since most of the users will want this information.

This list makes a useful quick-reference tool, but to get the fullest use from the films, more detailed indexing is necessary and this will involve the detailed analysis of the various scenes and people filmed. In the libraries of film studios it is the practice to analyse photographs and films in the greatest detail possible —from experience the film librarian knows that at any moment may come a demand for an accurate picture of an Italian telephone in use in 1932, for the façade of a barber's shop in a gold-rush town of the '49, or for a full-length portrait of Verdi. In the home, indexing to such an extent is unnecessary, but even so it is worth a little trouble to be able to put one's hand on a scene showing a child at a certain age or at a certain moment, and to be able to review rapidly all that one has about a person or a place.

On family films, therefore, the chief interests are:

(1) Persons
(2) Places
(3) Situations and Events

and any film to be indexed should be scrutinised with these three points of view in mind. For the purpose of indexing each fifty or hundred feet of film should be identified by a letter of the alphabet, so that the approximate position of each scene can be judged. Thus a scene which shows John watching a carnival in Falmouth would have the following entries:

JOHN (10)	Falmouth Holiday (c)
FALMOUTH HIGH ST.	Falmouth Holiday (c)
CARNIVAL	Falmouth Holiday (c)

and, whether one wanted a picture of John at the age of 10,

or all the pictures of carnivals in the collection, they would be ready to hand. For further abbreviation the number of the film can be substituted for the title, in which case the third entry should be expanded:

CARNIVAL (Falmouth)   14 (c)

In any extensive collection it may be necessary to include details of size of film, positive or negative, source, and name of the person taking each scene. But the index need not be elaborate, and is best kept on loose-leaf slips in a binder so that it can readily be handled when most of the room is in darkness.

Where collections of films are being built up for the purpose of hobbies or research, the indexing must be more thorough. A bird observer, for example, would require details of type of bird, exact place where seen, date and time, weather, and other circumstances, and he might want analytical entries under several of these headings. An enthusiastic gardener, making frequent shots of the growth of particular varieties of plants would need a record of date, time, weather, temperature, and any additional circumstances which might have occurred since taking the last shot. Whatever the type of film made, in framing the rules for its indexing the point to keep in mind is the purposes for which the index will be used, and only to make those entries which will be needed at any time in the future.

If, on the other hand, the collection is one of films made commercially or by other people, the initial list should include a description of each film giving some at least of the following details:

Manufacturer or studio
Place and date made
Width; positive or negative; silent, sound, etc.
Length
Cast; producer; director, etc.
Synopsis

and where the collector is likely to want detailed information on a particular aspect, analytical entries should be made:

CLAIR, René
   Le million   23
   Sous les toits de Paris   27

The possibilities of indexing films are innumerable, and by the careful selection of headings it often happens that new viewpoints and parallels present themselves leading to a greater appreciation of the film and its development.

For those who would like to study the cataloguing and indexing of films, a short but excellent treatise has recently been published: *Rules for Use in the Cataloguing Department of the National Film Archive*, 5th edition, 1960. (The British Film Institute, 81 Dean Street, London, W.1. 5s. or 60c.). The pioneer work of the Institute is well known, and here two experts show exactly how films are recorded in the greatest film library in the world.

Indexing
shadows
on a screen

*The place to begin looking in an index is under
the heading coming first to mind.*
E. J. CRANE and CHARLES L. BERNIER:
Indexing and Index-Searching

THE ILLUSTRATIONS on the following pages demonstrate an important and little-known aspect of indexing which is being developed in great detail at the present time. Mr. David Grenfell, former Chief Cataloguer of the National Film Archive, has selected from his unique catalogue of news films three examples of the kind of work that is being done in this field. In the illustrations the large card (8 in. by 5 in.) represents the main entry, while the smaller cards (5 in. by 3 in.) are the index entries.

The first example, the Pathé Gazette for 8th February, 1912, gives the main title BELFAST, the sub-title THE CHURCHILL MEETING, and the individual titles *Scenes and incidents . . .* and *Arrival of Lord Pirrie. . . .* The words following the individual titles are descriptive notes supplied by the National Film Archive after scrutinising each shot, and the figures following in brackets indicate the footage of the film. Thus the complete film is 81 feet long, it is on 35mm. film, is silent, and is a positive copy. In the index entries to this film it will be noticed that a great deal of research has been done to identify completely the people appearing in the film: names, titles and dates have been amplified and checked, and a subject entry BELFAST—Political Meetings has been added. The headings of all these index entries are also typed on the back of the main entry card, so that they can be amended or withdrawn at any time.

Similarly the cards for the extra edition of the German news film KINO KRIEGSHAU of October, 1914, show much helpful additional matter—particularly in the final three lines on the main card, where the cataloguer notes the inclusion of the statue (a detail which may be required at some time). At the top of the index cards classification symbols as well as subject headings are included—both are noted on the back of the main card.

The third example is particularly interesting since it is a fragment of an 1897 film. From research the cataloguer has decided that the complete film was called TWENTY YEARS AGO, and has put this title in parenthesis to indicate that it does not appear on the actual film. The heading *or this ? ? ?* is on the film, which starts at foot 120. At the end of the main entry the figure (56) indicates that the National Film Archive possesses only 56 feet of this film, i.e. feet 120–76.

The value of indexing of this kind is apparent: such detail adds immensely to the pictorial sources for biography, history, social research, the chronicling of fashion, etc. Readers who are particularly interested in this work will be pleased to read Mr. Grenfell's 'The cataloguing of newsfilms in the National Film Library' (*University Film Journal*, Summer 1955, pages 26 to 32), and to examine the *Rules for use in the Cataloguing Department of the National Film Archive* (5th edition. London, British Film Institute, 1960. vii, 46 pages) with its eighteen pages of further examples, and *The Arrangement of Film Catalogues. Recommendations made by the Cataloguing Committee of the British Film Institute* (London, British Film Institute, 1951, ii, 5 pages).

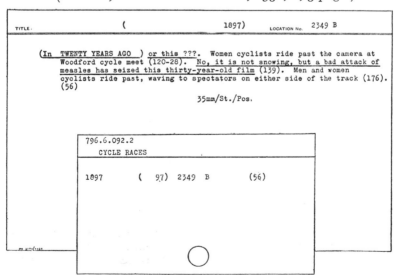

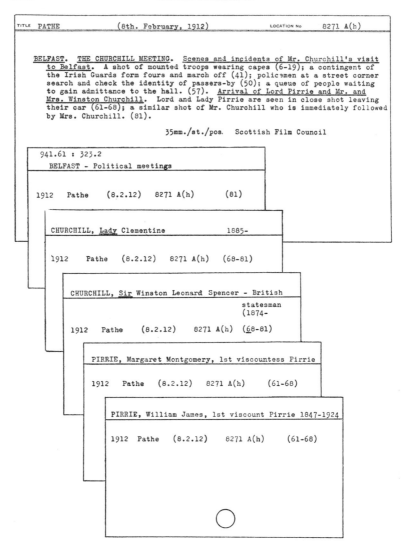

TITLE PATHE   (8th. February, 1912)   LOCATION No   8271 A(h)

BELFAST. THE CHURCHILL MEETING. Scenes and incidents of Mr. Churchill's visit to Belfast. A shot of mounted troops wearing capes (6-19); a contingent of the Irish Guards form fours and march off (41); policemen at a street corner search and check the identity of passers-by (50); a queue of people waiting to gain admittance to the hall. (57). Arrival of Lord Pirrie and Mr. and Mrs. Winston Churchill. Lord and Lady Pirrie are seen in close shot leaving their car (61-68); a similar shot of Mr. Churchill who is immediately followed by Mrs. Churchill. (81).

35mm./st./pos.   Scottish Film Council

941.61 : 323.2
    BELFAST - Political meetings

1912   Pathe   (8.2.12)   8271 A(h)   (81)

CHURCHILL, Lady Clementine   1885-

1912   Pathe   (8.2.12)   8271 A(h)   (68-81)

CHURCHILL, Sir Winston Leonard Spencer - British
                                      statesman
                                      (1874-
1912   Pathe   (8.2.12)   8271 A(h)   (68-81)

PIRRIE, Margaret Montgomery, 1st viscountess Pirrie

1912   Pathe   (8.2.12)   8271 A(h)   (61-68)

PIRRIE, William James, 1st viscount Pirrie 1847-1924

1912   Pathe   (8.2.12)   8271 A(h)   (61-68)

NB   Only the underlined words on the main card actually appear on the film; the remainder are annotations prepared by the cataloguers as they scrutinise the film. The smaller cards index the event and the personalities involved, but there is scope for further indexing under such headings as Irish Guards, Cavalry, etc.

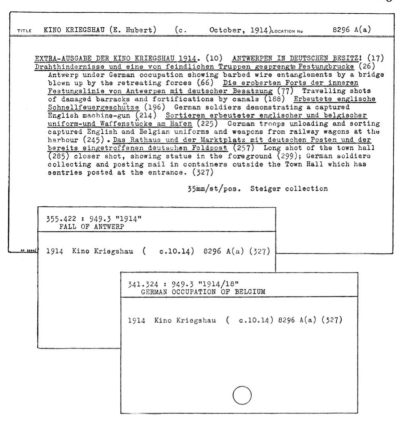

TITLE KINO KRIEGSHAU (E. Hubert)   (c.   October, 1914) LOCATION No   8296 A(a)

EXTRA-AUSGABE DER KINO KRIEGSHAU 1914. (10) ANTWERPEN IN DEUTSCHEN BESITZ! (17)
Drahthindernisse und eine von feindlichen Truppen gesprengte Festungbrucke (26)
Antwerp under German occupation showing barbed wire entanglements by a bridge
blown up by the retreating forces (66) Die eroberten Forts der inneren
Festungslinie von Antwerpen mit deutscher Besatzung (77) Travelling shots
of damaged barracks and fortifications by canals (188) Erbeutete englische
Schnellfeuergeschütze (196) German soldiers demonstrating a captured
English machine-gun (214) Sortieren erbeuteter englischer und belgischer
uniform-und Waffenstücke am Hafen (225) German troops unloading and sorting
captured English and Belgian uniforms and weapons from railway wagons at the
harbour (245) . Das Rathaus und der Marktplatz mit deutschen Posten und der
bereits eingetroffenen deutschen Feldpost (257) Long shot of the town hall
(285) closer shot, showing statue in the foreground (299); German soldiers
collecting and posting mail in containers outside the Town Hall which has
sentries posted at the entrance. (327)

                         35mm/st/pos. Steiger collection

355.422 : 949.3 "1914"
   FALL OF ANTWERP

1914 Kino Kriegshau (c.10.14) 8296 A(a) (327)

341.324 : 949.3 "1914/18"
   GERMAN OCCUPATION OF BELGIUM

1914 Kino Kriegshau (c.10.14) 8296 A(a) (327)

NB   Free translations of the film captions are interspersed with
     annotations. Here again there is scope for additional analytical
     indexing under such headings as Antwerp: Town Hall; Ant-
     werp: Market Place; German Soldiers; etc. The class numbers
     give priority to military and political aspects, but these could
     be developed to include entries under the history of World
     War I.

The
indexing of
periodicals

*Of course one has to have an
Index.*

STEPHEN LEACOCK

IN THESE TIMES an increasing amount of material—such as important discoveries, theories and research—make their first public appearance in the columns of periodicals; they may reach books for the first time some years later. The acknowledgments and bibliographies in books frequently refer to earlier publications in periodical form, and often the only information on recent subjects is found in articles in periodicals, or the Transactions and Proceedings of learned societies or research associations. Certainly, even with established subjects with a considerable literature in book form, it is necessary to consult the periodical literature on the subject in order to correct or adjust the ideas in books by the newer discoveries or research. In such subjects, for example, as archaeology, literature, art, etc.—apart from scientific and technical subjects in which knowledge is developing daily and changing rapidly—the advances in recent years have been sufficiently remarkable to make many of the older books partly out of date.

It is therefore essential to have as complete and as detailed a key to periodical literature as possible. There is a large number of published indexes to periodicals today, and they cover a fair amount of the important periodical literature of the twentieth century. Their treatment, however, is purely general, since they must of necessity appeal to a fairly wide public, and very often their degree of detail is not sufficient for the specialist's requirements. Moreover, the number of periodicals published today is vast. The annual edition of *The Newspaper Press Directory* (Benn) lists some five thousand five hundred newspapers and periodicals published in Great Britain alone. The chief directory of the United States of America, Ayer's (annual) *Directory of Periodicals*, lists some twenty-three thousand published in the

United States and Canada. Yet neither of these is by any means complete. The published general indexes to periodicals can cover only a small proportion of them.

It is true that many periodicals publish their own indexes, but too often these are mere contents lists which do not attempt to analyse the contents of the articles in detail, or even to enter the titles under suitable subject-headings. It is rare that these so-called indexes are compiled by experienced indexers, and very few of them cover more than a single year at a time, while most of them are not compiled on scientific principles.

In some subjects, learned societies and research bodies have attempted to overcome the lack of good indexes by compiling and publishing detailed indexes in their own fields. The most successful ventures in this field are those in such subjects as Chemistry, Medicine, Engineering, and other technical and scientific subjects. Even so, the specialist libraries in these subjects continue to compile their own indexes as well, both because they need still more detailed information and, what is more important, they require indexes compiled from their own point of view.

The reason for this last point may not be immediately obvious. A research institution concerned with the motor industry will however have a very different interest in an article on paints and varnishes from that of the British Colour Council. The points of interest to the one are quite different from those which appeal to the other. It is this factor which forces organisations to index for themselves the more important articles, and it means that any central system of indexing must be supplemented by individual indexing for outstanding items.

The indexing of periodicals is based on the same principles as those for the indexing of books, but it involves a stricter discipline, a wider knowledge and unswerving consistency. It is comparatively easy to make a good and consistent index to a book, for it is a single operation which can be carried out in a reasonably short space of time, and it is not too large a task to be carried out by one person. An index to periodicals is however an operation carried out over a long period—possibly performed by several people—and it covers a greater amount and variety of material, generally speaking. Continuative indexing means that the principles on which the index is compiled in one month must be strictly followed in all further instalments if the reader is to discover quickly and easily *all* the material on his subject. If this is not done, there is a danger that some users of the index may miss important items: for instance, in one famous annual index of periodicals, articles on printing are entered under the heading PRINTING in some issues, and under the heading TYPOGRAPHY in others. Thus the research worker who is looking up what has been published on this subject must waste time in looking under both headings if he is not certain whether the entries will appear under one or other heading.

It is therefore essential to build up a standard list of subject-headings to ensure uniformity in every instalment of the index, but this will not prevent or preclude revision. Indeed, the addition of new subjects, and the alteration of headings will be essential from time to time. For example, the popular phrase Infantile Paralysis has almost given place to the difficult yet thoroughly familiar medical term Poliomyelitis, and while entries in pre-war years might have been made under the first of these terms, contemporary entries might be thought better placed under the second. Developments of this kind are taking place all the time, but alterations should not be made until the new name has become firmly established, and references from the old names should always be made.

Changes of this kind also enable scattered headings to be brought closer together. Thus a number of articles on secondary schools could be entered under the heading SECONDARY SCHOOLS, but they could, on the other hand, be brought into juxtaposition with the main heading SCHOOLS and other related subjects, by the process of transposing the heading—SCHOOLS, Secondary. Reversals of similar headings would have the effect of bringing many of the related headings within a fairly close range:

SCHOOLS		
SCHOOLS, Comprehensive	*with*	COMPREHENSIVE SCHOOLS
SCHOOLS, Primary	*references*	PRIMARY SCHOOLS
SCHOOLS, Secondary	*from*	SECONDARY SCHOOLS
SCHOOLS, Technical		TECHNICAL SCHOOLS

On the other hand, where it is felt that such a concentration of entries is undesirable the transposal can be dropped, and the headings in the right-hand column used as main headings, the necessary general reference being made from those in the left-hand list.

Once a standard list of subject-headings suitable for the purpose has been compiled, the way is clear to begin the actual indexing of periodicals. Each article to be indexed should be read through and the main index heading written above the article in pencil, other index headings being written against the relevant passages. When all the articles and other items in the given periodical have been treated in this way, the index slips can be made out. If the same periodicals are indexed week after week, it is economical to have slips printed with the name of the individual periodicals—or to use different coloured slips for different periodicals—so that the repetition of writing or typing the name of the periodical in each entry is avoided. Whatever method is used, the name of the periodical should be abbreviated in accordance with the recommendations of the *World List of Scientific Periodicals* . . . 4th edition (Butterworth, 1963–5), or those of the British Standard Institution's *Bibliographical References* (British Standard 1629: 1950), so that identification is facilitated both in this country and overseas. The subject-heading is then written at the top, and below is written the title of the article, the name of the author (if known), and a reference to the periodical concerned:

HYDROPONICS
Soilless culture in winter. Arthur Hamilton.
Jnl R. Hort. S., 28: 153–7. Je 50

It will be seen that by this system much information is given in comparatively little space. After the abbreviated name of the periodical, the volume number is given, followed by the page-reference, and an abbreviated date. Additional entries can be made, were necessary, under the author's name, distinctive titles, additional subjects, and important series titles if readers are likely to want to read a complete series of articles.

One of the most serious problems of periodical indexing is

the difficulty of alphabetisation. Apart from encyclopaedias and dictionaries, the average book index presents few problems of alphabetising, since the fact that most books are limited to one or more aspects of a subject implies that an individual word will rarely be used in two or more meanings. But in periodical indexing the same word may occur in many different connections. For example, the name Cyclops is used in various volumes of the *Readers' Guide to Periodical Literature* as a name in classical mythology, the name of a naval collier, and the name of a species in zoology.

The H. W. Wilson Company of New York has a detailed set of instructions on the arrangement of entries. The 'word by word' system is used, and if the same word is used in different senses, those denoting persons are placed first, followed by places and then subjects, and lastly titles. Thus:

> Castle, Arthur
> Castle, (Durham)
> Castle (subject)
> *Castle, The*

The arrangement of entries under their headings is also strictly controlled. Under any heading the general references are placed first. These are followed by geographical divisions, arranged alphabetically. Alphabetical sub-arrangement is abandoned in favour of chronological arrangement under historical subjects. Such rules are based on sound common sense and immense experience, and are well worth careful study before embarking on a periodicals index of one's own. In this connection, the American Library Association's *Rules for Filing Catalog Cards* (revised edition, Chicago, American Library Association, 1968), will be found of great assistance in solving difficulties encountered in the larger indexes.

If the periodicals index is duplicated or printed for circulation at frequent intervals, the original slips should be retained to enable cumulated annual or multi-annual volumes to be compiled. They will of course require considerable editing for these cumulations, for the larger the index the more need there is for detailed sub-division, and for cross-references, while the problems of sub-arrangement increase rapidly with the size.

There are many excellent examples on which such cumulations can be based by carefully studying their technique, and a visit to any large public or university reference library will enable these to be compared in detail.

Compiling and arranging a bibliography

*A very profitable Index
to the family.*

WILLIAM HINDE

ONE OF THE MOST USEFUL TYPES of index which can be compiled is a guide to the literature of a subject. If it is an informal and simple affair it is known as a reading list; and, if it is scientifically compiled, it is known as a bibliography. In either case, if it is the product of experience and good judgment it may save many another person much time and may introduce him to sources whose existence he might otherwise never have known. Whether bibliography or reading list it is quite often arranged alphabetically by author, but this is the least useful method, and it is preferable that entries be arranged by subjects in a logical order. This then becomes an index to the subject, and the usual alphabetical arrangement familiar in general indexes gives place to a classified order, although this in turn may have an alphabetical index of its own.

The first step is to compile slips for all the different items—books, pamphlets, periodicals and periodical articles, illustrations, maps, plans, posters, abstracts, etc.—which it is desired to record. Each slip should be made out in a standard form: author, title, publisher, date, and page and/or chapter references, for books; author, title, periodical, volume number, page references, date, for periodical articles; and so on. Each entry should give information in exactly the same order so that the time and patience of the reader is not wasted. Under the title *Bibliographical References* (British Standard 1629: 1950), the British Standards Institution has published a very interesting and helpful guide on the proper framing of these entries in a form which is recognised internationally. When the slips have been compiled—and no slip should bear references to more than one item—they should be arranged in alphabetical order and any duplications eliminated. They should also be compared to ensure uniformity, for some authors sign their names in different forms at different periods, some journals will be found to have changed their titles or volume numbering slightly, and other small inconsistencies will come to light.

The slips should then be re-sorted in subject order and slips with subject-headings and sub-headings added. The subject groups should then be arranged in logical order. It will now be necessary to consider each group in turn and decide what annotations should be added to each entry to show what contribution it makes to the subject, what standard of preliminary knowledge it demands from its readers, and to show whether there are illustrations, tables, indexes or other information which are of special significance. Even the briefest of notes is of assistance to the reader in helping him to decide which entries best meet his requirements. It may be found that it is possible to add a symbol to each which will sufficiently indicate the type of material represented: reference work, general or popular treatment, elementary introduction, intermediate textbook, advanced work or specialist monograph, etc.

Each slip should then be given a running number for reference. Finally the bibliography should be read through thoroughly to ensure that each entry is clear and that the annotations are apt and sufficiently full to ensure that the reader will gain a good idea from the entry itself whether or not he wishes to examine the material described. The bibliography is then ready for typing.

When the typing is completed, the slips should be checked with the manuscript, for it is essential that all references should be accurate: an ambiguous or inaccurate reference may cause the reader to waste much time in discovering the correct material, or may even prevent his referring to it. The slips should then be re-sorted in alphabetical order. They will then form the basis of an index to the bibliography. When the slips are in alphabetical order they should be examined to determine the need for additional entries. These will consist of extra subject-headings and references, title entries wherever there is a significant or memorable title, and references from joint-authors, alternative forms of names (such as the part of a double-barrelled name not used for entry purposes, sub-titles, etc.). To the slips containing subject-headings will have to be added the reference numbers covering those subjects, and reference numbers will also have to be added to any additional entries made. The slips must then be edited: that is, all words and material not required for the index must be eliminated. The index is then ready for typing. Afterwards the typescript must be checked carefully with the slips.

Reference numbers to individual items are preferable to page references in the index, since it is difficult to identify a reference to a particular item on the condensed page of a bibliography, if no more particular reference is made.

In the work of compiling a bibliography much depends on the type of material listed. A bibliography of modern material on scientific or technical subjects is fairly straightforward, since few details are required of the make-up of a particular book or pamphlet. If, however, the bibliography includes or mainly consists of rare or old books, much more bibliographical information is required, and much valuable guidance can be obtained on the procedure to be followed from the late J. D. Cowley's *Bibliographical Description and Cataloguing* (Grafton, 1948), which ranks with R. B. McKerrow's *Bibliography* as one of the few literary classics on the study and handling of books.

There are also two further items which provide considerable assistance in the preparation of bibliographies. A. W. Pollard's *The Arrangement of Bibliographies*, first published in the *Library* (2nd series, volume 10, 1909, pages 168–87), has long been recognised as the classic on the subject, and has since been reprinted separately by the Association of Assistant Librarians. The National Council of Social Service, in its Local History Series, has published *The Compilation of County Bibliographies* (December, 1948), which includes an excellent classification scheme for county bibliographies compiled by E. H. Cordeaux and D. H. Merry of the Bodleian Library. An invaluable reference book is J. Carter's *ABC for Book-Collectors* (5th edition, Rupert Hart-Davis, 1968).

Breaking the
sound barrier

An index is an array of symbols, systematically arranged, together with a reference from each symbol to the physical location of the item symbolized.

MORTIMER TAUBE: Studies in
coordinate indexing

CAN SOUNDS BE ADEQUATELY INDEXED? This is a problem which is being increasingly studied by some of our best brains and, in some fields at least, considerable advances have already been made. For instance, the indexing of musical themes has been put on a scientific footing with remarkable success. But there are other types of sound which need this kind of treatment and it is in the motion-picture world that most work has been done so far. The question arises over the establishment of an effective system for classifying and filing the sound effect tracks which have been recorded for a film in production so that they can be discovered and used again whenever they are required. One of the most interesting experiments in this work was carried out at the Shell Film Unit under the direction of Miss Peggy Dowling: although the technique is still largely in the experimental stage, sufficient progress has been made for the system to bear general examination.

At the Shell Film Unit the original effects negatives of completed documentary films are passed to the Sound Library, where they are examined on a sound head and the individual sound effects are isolated for separate storage. Each sound effect is classified and indexed, and the rolls of film are then stored in metal containers, both film and container being labelled with a note of the contents.

The classification is done by the Universal Decimal Classification, a conventional classification much used by scientific libraries throughout the world. Thus a typical classified entry would read:

621.733.4   NS 226
Hammering metal on an anvil
Roll 5. 8 ZF 56551–56639   Repeated medium pitch and tempo,
                                             resonant metallic knocking

In this entry 621.733.4 represents the U.D.C. number for the mechanical process, NS 226 is the accession number of the film, Roll 5 identifies the actual roll of film bearing this sound effect, and 8 ZF 56551–56639, which is the progressive number printed on the edge of the negative every foot by the Laboratories, also identifies and assists in estimating the actual length of the footage. The description 'Repeated medium pitch . . .' is an analytical description which is based on the following system of examination:

(a) *Category*   such as billiard ball, single-cylinder test engine, etc.
(b) *Frequency*   constant, intermittent, repeated, irregular, continuous.
(c) *Pitch*   high, medium, low.
(d) *Speed*   mostly applicable to music, banging noises, etc.
(e) *Type*   such as thuds, bangs, clangs, clatters, whines, etc.
(f) *Resonance*   echo, or no echo.

An alphabetical index of subjects used in the Universal Decimal Classification, as applied to this Library, is also kept. So far, the procedure is comparatively conventional, but the Unit has an additional index which is unique and has great significance. The key to this index is item (e) above in which sound effects are described by type: the additional index provides a special approach to the sound effects by entries under the main groups which, at present, are given under the following headings:

Bangs	Metallic knocks and taps
Beats	Rattle (falling objects)
Bubbling	Ripping
Buzz	Roar
Chatter (Mechanical)	Rumble
Chinks	Running Liquids
Clangs	Shushing (such as windmill sails)
Clanks	Slams

Clicks	Splash
Cracks	Squeaks
Crash	Throb
Hiss	Thuds
Hum	Twang
Mellow knocks	Whine

It is clear that different film libraries might add to these headings, but all the basic sounds are here. The contrast with the conventional classification entries is notable: thus, under the classification number 621.873, we find:

621.873   NS 232
Crane effects
Roll 1. 39 YC 89235–89605   Metallic throbbing and whining of motor
     2. 86 ZC 58436–58531   lifting and lowering heavy metal plate
     3. 53 ZS 92525–92578   chains dropping; metallic clinks
     4. 86 ZC 58252–58326   metallic clang of crane hooks

Consider now the entries to be found under a typical group heading such as WHINE:

621.313.12   NS 311
Turbines in electric power house
Roll 3. 8 YF 39303–39425   High-pitched continuous whine
621.313.12   NS 311
Electric generator running
Roll 1. 125 YF 18500–18631   Constant medium-pitched whine
621.631   NS 311
Large electric fan starting and running
Roll 2. 247 YF 77484–77548   Constant whine increasing in pitch
621.924   NS 232   –
Grinding metal
Roll 5. 86 ZC 58372–58435   High-pitched whine
621.944   NS 309
Steel rolling mill effects
Roll 1. 247 YF 77173–77246   Milling aluminium at speed—constant medium-pitched pressurised whine
     2. 247 YF 77250–77332   ditto

With such an index it is possible to offer a large variety of individual noises which would be difficult to discover from the classified index alone. Thus the search for a sound representing catching and kicking a football would be concentrated under the heading THUDS, while that for smashing a ball bearing (a sound which resembles a rifle shot) would be made under BANGS. More complex sounds such as the sound of hobnail boots on gravel on a clear cold night would be rather more difficult to treat in this fashion, but the establishment of a further category of background noises is already under consideration. Under some headings a wider choice becomes available: thus, under CLICKS we find sounds of turnstiles, donkey engines, and winches.

The indexer's approach to the indexing of sound would so far appear to be a choice of (*a*) conventional library classification; (*b*) classification by materials (leather, wood, metal, etc.); (*c*) by actual objects (winches, steel rolling mills, etc.); (*d*) types of noise (thuds, bangs, etc.), or—as in the examples given above—a combination of all four. Certainly, the system just described has wider applications, especially in the field of concrete music, and in that of animated sound on film (see *Science and Film*, June and December, 1955, pages 27–30 and 18–35 respectively). Still another choice however is available through the use of co-ordinate indexing, to which the Shell Film Unit's system bears some (though an unconscious) relationship, and in the following two chapters a summary is given of one of the most revolutionary developments in recent indexing in which the use of co-ordinate (or Uniterm) headings has broken an equally difficult barrier in the field of highly technical document indexing.

Business
indexing

Since the Letters are not Indexed,
I cannot point out all the places.
WODROW: Correspondence

THE SCENE IS THE BOARD MEETING of a large organisation. Under the heading of 'Any other business' at the end of a long afternoon session, a member has raised the comparatively unimportant point of the non-appointment of a candidate for a junior position on the staff. To clear up a trivial detail the Chairman sends for the original letter of application which, after some delay, proves not to be available. After some aimless discussion the matter is postponed until the next meeting. Subsequent investigation shows that the letter was not lost: it had been filed under the name of the firm at present employing the applicant—who had used official notepaper for his purpose— instead of under his own name. The fault was not, in fact, one of filing but one of indexing; the result however was the same— loss of time and delay in action.

One of the most persistent problems in even the smallest office is the efficient control of correspondence, reports, memoranda, directives, etc. In the largest organisations it is still the subject of much experiment. For instance, the registration and routing of correspondence and the writing of replies are all matters which have long been subject to a rigid routine, but the ultimate indexing and filing of letters and the carbon copies of replies so that they can be found again are still open to many variations in procedure. The difficulty lies in the complex nature of much business correspondence: a letter from one man to another, affirming that he is alive and well, can have only one indexing reference—the correspondent's own name! If, on the other hand, he writes concerning such matters as his property, a life insurance, a new invention, etc., an additional indexing reference may become necessary since the letter may be referred to later not by the man's name (which may have been forgotten) but by the subject-matter of the letter. When the correspondence is no longer between one man and another, but between members of two organisations, whose corporate interests may cover many varied spheres, the complexities grow. Thus a large organisation may consist of many different units (factories, offices, retail outlets, concessions, agencies, etc.) in several countries—in addition to various subsidiaries—and its products may cover a wide variety of items. Double this by assuming that its correspondents are equally comprehensive in their activities, and the necessities of accurate and detailed indexing become a matter of the utmost importance.

Indexing is so important in such matters since a letter may be demanded from many different points of view. Thus it may be referred to by the organisation's name, by the name of the individual writer, by the name of a subsidiary firm or by the geographical location or the local name of an office or a factory, or by the subject of one of several points raised in the letter. The art of satisfactorily indexing such items lies in being able to estimate correctly all the various ways in which reference may be made to a document, and in being able to codify such ideas so that the approach to any individual item can be made by *any* member of the staff without loss of time.

It is not the purpose of this book to discuss in detail the vast subject of office filing, although filing systems are so much bound up with the methods of indexing on which they depend. It must be emphasised however that whatever filing system is chosen must rely on the efficiency of the indexing methods in force for the full exploitation of its contents, so that it is imperative to examine the organisation of the indexing at an early date. To do so, a preliminary survey of the whole problem is essential, and this must be based on two points:

(1) who is likely to use the files of correspondence, reports, inter-office memoranda, directives, etc.?

(2) under what headings is each of these items likely to be demanded?

In existing organisations these can be determined by an intensive study of day-to-day use of the files and of the degree of success and speed with which demands can be met. In new organisations it is possible to begin with very detailed indexing based on an estimate of all possible requirements, and to reduce the number and types of references as the result of actual experience shows which kinds of entries can safely be eliminated.

The average business letter embodies the following points which are worthy of consideration for possible index entries:

(a) the name of the organisation writing the letter

(b) any other name (such as a former name) under which the organisation conducts its business

(c) the name of the individual writer where he himself—or his official position—is of particular interest to the organisation to which he is writing

(d) the names of persons and/or other organisations mentioned in the text of the letter

(e) the subject matter(s) of the letter—including names, trade-names or types of products, etc.

(f) the geographical territory—names of countries, cities, regions, etc., where these have their own importance from such points of view as development of sales territories, etc.

With regard to (a) it is important to note that it may be desirable in the case of a subsidiary firm to create at least a general cross-reference to the main organisation, and similar considerations relate to branch offices and factories, individual agencies and independent representatives, etc. In the case of (b) the necessity for such cross-references is even more important. The correspondent, in the case of (c), may well be significant in his own right, since he may be a director of several other companies, or may hold office in international, national or local professional or trade organisations. Item (d) is of varying importance: thus, in a solicitor's office the names of people mentioned in the body of a letter—defendant's counsel and their clients, interested parties, etc.—may be of significance years later in connection with other legal cases and proceedings. It is not necessary to elaborate on item (e), but for (f) it may be said that in some organisations it may be important to index more thoroughly under territories than under any other item: thus, in the case of a wholesale firm engaged on extending its activities in several different cities, it may be necessary at short notice to study all the correspondence and other documents relating to a particular area in order to reach a policy decision.

Without fear of serious opposition, it may be stated that few organisations enter upon or, having done so, maintain a system of indexing embodying all the points outlined in the preceding paragraph. Nor, in most cases, is it necessary—one or more items can safely be cut out according to individual needs. What is necessary, however, is to keep constantly in mind the widest possible range of indexing so that no desirable type of entry is omitted without thorough consideration.

Some business filing systems constitute in themselves the main index: for instance, the most usual practice of filing correspondence under the names of the correspondents provides in itself a crude coverage of items (*a*), (*b*) and (*c*)—crude, in that unless it is furnished with cross-references for alternative forms of names, branches, subsidiaries, agencies, etc., much important material will be overlooked from time to time. By itself it will certainly not cover items (*d*), (*e*) and (*f*), nor will cross-references in the files themselves be any acceptable solution for, in the long run, they will prove too cumbersome. The creation of a subsidiary index, usually in the form of a visible index or on cards, becomes necessary if these items are to be satisfactorily indexed. In any case, direct filing of this kind is fraught with indexing and filing difficulties. Few names of business organisations are straightforward from the point of view of people (and, in this case, the vast majority of the world's population) who are unfamiliar with the problems of complex alphabetisation. Consider in this connection the names of the following organisations taken at random from a current London telephone directory:

> The Elof Hansson Agency Ltd.
> F. & C. Engineering Works Ltd.
> First National City Bank of New York.
> Geliot-Whitman & Co.
> Gilbert-Ash Ltd.
> Greenwood's & Airvac Ventilating Co. Ltd.
> K. Harvey's Office Equipment.

It is no exaggeration to say that the filing clerk may well hesitate before deciding at which point in the alphabet the relative

correspondence should be indexed and filed. Reference to
material relating to such names as these is equally difficult, and
there are always possibilities of misfiling wherever new or un-
trained staff are employed. Thus both filing and tracing items
slow up the to detriment of the everyday procedure of the
business.

Some of the more popular filing systems in operation nowadays largely overcome this difficulty by combining alphabetical
filing of this kind with the use of code numbers or signals which
help to identify the individual organisations beyond any doubt.
Whether such adjuncts are used or not, the preliminary intervention of an experienced member of the staff who can consistently decide under which heading each item is to be filed
is essential, and implies also the existence of a master [authority]
list of decisions concerning suitable headings to which reference
may be made by all who wish to make use of the files.

The very existence of master indexes of this kind has occasioned in some organisations the abandoning of alphabetical in
favour of numerical filing, with its advantages of greater
accuracy in filing and in speed of reference. In such systems
each correspondent, whether corporate or individual, is awarded
a number and this number is stamped or written on each
document recorded as emanating from that correspondent. The
items are then filed under their appropriate number in chronological order of receipt (latest item foremost) and, if more
specific reference is needed, an individual number is given to
each letter, etc. Thus, if Messrs. George Brown & Sons Ltd.,
of Cardiff, are represented in this filing system by the number
1238, the symbol 1238/621 would indicate that the letter in
question is the 621st letter in the file relating to that firm.

Here analytical indexing is simplified and complexities of
subject-matter, etc., can easily be overcome. For example, in
the case of a letter from Messrs. George Brown & Sons relating
to the supply of shipments of steel to its factory in Rotherham,
the main index entry for the firm would cover *all* letters from
that source. Additional index entries, all bearing the number
of the letter, can be made at such points as may be thought
necessary. The resulting entries might well be as over page,
with as many more entries for subsidiary points as are likely
to be referred to from time to time. In such a system as this, the

BROWN, George, & Sons Ltd., Cardiff

1238

19.12.57	620
20.12.57	621
21.12.57	622

STEEL

1001	*1238*	*1569*	*1632*
301	620	704	158
359	622		353
			358

ROTHERHAM FACTORY

705	*1238*	*1569*	*1632*	*1825*
244	622	704	353	476
246			358	477

KEIGHTLEY, James

Mg. Dr., George Brown & Sons Ltd.

Cardiff

1238: 135, 246, 408, 622

considerable advantages of co-ordinate indexing—as described in the next chapter are obvious. But it must be admitted that while this system has the paramount advantage of accuracy, filing is delayed slightly owing to the need for making index entries, and weeding of files becomes difficult owing to the necessity for cancelling entries on the individual index cards. The ultimate microfilming of items which are to be destroyed would however overcome this particular disadvantage, since no cancellation of index entries would then be necessary. The great disadvantage of this system is, however, that approach is indirect, since reference must first be made to the index.

Co-ordinate indexing

It is easy enough to make an index, as it is to make a broom of odds and ends, as rough as oat straw; but to make an index tied up tight, and that will sweep well into corners, isn't so easy,

JOHN RUSKIN

ONE OF THE MOST EXCITING experiments in indexing in this generation is the process invented by Dr. Mortimer Taube and his associates in Documentation Incorporated. Indexers have long been aware of the highly haphazard nature of conventional indexing which largely depends for its success on the degree of similarity of approach reached by the indexer and the user of his index. Thus if both indexer and reader hit upon the same subject-heading when thinking of a given topic all is well; if they think of it on different lines then the reader is dependent on the indexer's provision of sufficient references to cover all the possible alternatives under which a reasonable man might expect to find some kind of entry. Thus, if the subject is Atomic Powered Rockets it is possible that different readers may look under one or more of the following headings:

Artificial Meteors	Satellite Rockets
Earth Satellites	Solar Rockets
Rockets, Atomic Powered	

But all this means in any detailed conventional indexing that the labour, stationery and space involved are often out of all proportion to the results.

Other difficulties encountered in conventional indexing include the rapid growth of indexes, involving physical problems of handling and searching. There is in fact a geometrical progression in the slowing up of inserting entries and in the pace of reference as the index grows larger. And with this come increasingly difficult problems of alphabetisation, of subdivision, and of complex headings, together with the necessity to provide additional guiding aids. Then there are the problems of language, closely coupled with the comparative poverty of existing forms of description. It is, for instance, usually impossible to make a complete search for material under any headings which are used only as subdivisions to many different topics.

Dr. Taube and his colleagues have discovered a way which appears to be very promising for certain types of indexing based on the conception of the Uniterm System of Co-ordinate Indexing. The theory is that each title, each article, etc., can be reduced for indexing purposes to a number of basic ideas capable of being represented mostly by single terms.

In the Uniterm system each book, document or other item is numbered as it is received and, if a record is kept of the numbers registered each day or week, it is possible to gain an approximate idea of the date of any currently-published item from its serial number. The title, salient contents, etc., of the document to be indexed are then analysed into fundamental terms usually of one word each. These constitute the Uniterms and a separate card is made for each Uniterm. These cards need not be large: the standard catalogue card 3 in. by 5 in. (an approximate measurement—the international standard is 12.7 cm. by 7.5 cm.) is sufficient for all but the most detailed work. Each card allows sufficient space at the top for entering the Uniterm, and the remainder of the space is ruled vertically in ten columns representing the numbers 0 to 9. The serial numbers of relevant documents are entered in the columns of appropriate Uniterm cards according to the *last* digit—the purpose of the columns being merely to break up the numbers posted on the cards into roughly ten equal groups which, as will be seen later, not only makes the utmost use of available space, but also helps to speed up the finding of documents.

Let us take Herbert A. Simon's *Models of Man: Social and Rational* (New York, Wiley, 1957), which is a series of mathematical essays on rational human behaviour in a social setting. Assuming that for some purpose or other we wish to make a general reference to Chapter 7 which is called 'Mechanisms involved in pressures toward uniformity in groups., which is given the serial number 234, the Uniterm cards will be as shown overleaf.

MECHANISMS

0	1	2	3	4	5	6	7	8	9
			234						

PRESSURES

0	1	2	3	4	5	6	7	8	9
			234						

UNIFORMITY

0	1	2	3	4	5	6	7	8	9
			234						

GROUPS

0	1	2	3	4	5	6	7	8	9
			234						

If the next item to be indexed was Chapter 8: 'Mechanisms involved in group pressures on deviate-members', suitable Uniterms would be chosen and some of these would be Mechanisms, Pressures, etc., so that the number 235 would also appear on the cards for those terms.

It will be seen that however this chapter is referred to at a later date—and people's memories are often both inaccurate and shaky—the chances of discovering it by examining the Uniterm cards are high. The system of using an index compiled on Uniterm cards is simple: the subject enquiry is analysed into Uniterms and the appropriate cards are withdrawn from the file and compared. Numbers common to two or more cards indicate documents which are relevant to the subject: the presence of the same number on two or more cards indicates that the ideas they represent intersect—hence the name co-ordinate indexing. Since all the documents are kept in one numerical order, finding the actual items is straightforward. Nor is the comparison of the cards difficult since the numbers appear in each column in numerical order, so that to compare the same

K

column on three or more cards it is simply necessary to take
the numbers on the shortest of the columns and ascertain
whether they appear on the other cards. Thus, taking the first
two cards above and assuming that each now includes other
numbers:

MECHANISMS

0	1	2	3	4	5	6	7	8	9
10	21	32	13	234	125	36	47	28	99
150	91	242	63	344		56	57	128	109
170	121	292	73	354		76	97		119
240		302				326			339

PRESSURES

0	1	2	3	4	5	6	7	8	9
10	41	22	43	44	55	26	157	38	98
80	91	62	73	234	85		187	78	179
130	141	192	133	374	135		307	208	
	171			444			407		

Comparison of these two cards shows that the items numbered
91, 73 and 234 appear on both cards—readers may care to test
themselves on the amount of time needed for a thorough comparison though, to obtain a true record, it would be necessary
to use actual cards for the purpose.

Thus if all four salient terms are remembered correctly it is
probable that the exact document will be identified right away,
no matter in what order those terms are recalled. Even if only
one term is recalled the document will eventually be discovered,
while each additional term will narrow the search.

Compare now the fate of the searcher looking for such an
item in a conventional catalogue. Presumably the index entries
would be made on the following lines:

> Group uniformity
> Pressure groups
> Uniform conduct

In a small index it would therefore be possible to find the document just as easily if search were made under the words, Group,

Pressure, or Uniform. But in the vast indexes of many thousands of items for which this form of indexing is particularly designed, it would be possible to miss this chapter unless references or entries were also made under the headings:

Conduct, Uniformity of
Group pressures
Uniform behaviour

and, it will be noticed, that even so there is still no approach through the word Mechanisms which, although of subsidiary subject importance, has the powerful mnemonic value of being the first word of the title.

Thus four Uniterm cards will perform a better job than six conventional index entries. Moreover, in any clearly-defined subject field the number of separate Uniterms declines steadily as the number of documents indexed increases. In a British experiment in the indexing of 200 highly-technical aeronautical documents it was found that while the first fifty documents required 205 Uniterms, the next fifty needed only an additional 80 Uniterms, the following 87, and the final fifty only 62—a total of 429 Uniterms for 200 documents, which is less than the number of entries which would be needed in a conventional index. Again, in a parallel experiment in indexing 500 similar documents only 377 Uniterms were used, but in this case the indexing was not nearly as effective in its work. From a graph of the numbers of Uniterms used in the two experiments it was apparent that the increase in numbers tended to decline markedly after the first 150 documents indexed in both cases.

Some readers may well be apprehensive concerning the mass of serial numbers likely to appear on the more popular Uniterm cards. Here the experience gained in the two experiments may prove of interest: the most popular card—presumably a subject such as Aircraft or Flight—amassed 209 entries in one experiment and 126 in the other, but the next most popular had only 57 and 55 entries respectively, while the following five cards varied between 10 and 30, the remainder having 8 or less. A curve of these showed a gradient of no more than about 20 deg. In a very large-scale American experiment involving over 70,000 documents it was found that once the first eight thousand Uniterms have been chosen, the rate of addition of new terms falls off very rapidly, even where the subject matter of the documents is highly varied. Once forty or fifty thousand documents have been indexed, the addition of new Uniterms becomes very slow. The organisation conducting the experiment came to the conclusion that once ten thousand Uniterms have come into use, the additions consist almost entirely of highly specific names, such as new trade names and terms used to describe new equipment.

Of course, there are snags. Where the co-ordinate index deals with a comparatively small and specialised group of subjects in which each term has a well-understood and unambiguous meaning, few difficulties in the choice of terminology arise however large the index grows. But where the index covers a very wide subject-field in which, for instance, the term Pressure may refer—as in the example above—to Group Pressure—or to Pressure in the engineering sense, additional care must be taken to define the terms used to avoid irrelevant references. Again, it is not easy to break down some terms for the Uniterm system—for example, in the expression Loaded Wagon, the Uniterms Load and Wagon will not completely fulfil the intention of the original phrase. In such cases some users have elected to use terms consisting of two or three words where they express a specific idea, such as Aircraft Fire Control Systems. Again, synonyms must be dealt with by means of references, such as by referring from Acoustics to Sound.

One of the most important criticisms of the Uniterm system is that it deals better with enquiries for specialised items than with those for purely general subjects. Wherever purely general subjects are concerned it may be necessary to compare two or three cards containing many numbers, which means that there is a possibility of missing some of the relevant items through mere physical fatigue caused by prolonged scrutiny. This consideration would however apply in any circumstance—for example, in examining a library of 1,000 books concerned with Plastics for items referring to modern methods of strengthening plastic materials, the margin of error would be at least as large.

From the filing point of view, the Uniterm scheme is ideal— new additions are added at the end of the existing sequence, so that there is no need to leave space throughout the files for the insertion of items. Moreover the use of a numerical sequence means that no filing clerk, however junior, will have any doubts concerning where any particular item is to be filed nor where it is to be found. Guiding the files becomes a very simple matter of showing inclusive numbers every 100 documents or so, and control of the whole mechanical process of filing and searching and refiling is efficient and swift.

Co-ordinate indexing is still a comparatively new method which is subject to improvement and modification. It is not applicable to the construction of ordinary printed indexes to books, but its application to the organisation of large quantities of miscellaneous documents is clearly well worth considering, and future developments in its use are certain to be watched with intense interest by all who are faced with the problem of coping with rapidly increasing quantities of documents that must be made available for instant and constant use. Thus, in industry, commerce and scientific and technological research there is a permanent place for this type of system which meets the demand for speedy action, with a simple yet effective scheme that can be made infinitely expansible and flexible.

The
future

*Books with no indexes at all
are apparently written or published by egotists.*

LORENA GARLOCH

THE DEVELOPMENT OF THE CAPACITIES of computers, the
search for profitable by-products for the tapes prepared for film-
setting, and the growing realisation of the need for more speedy
indexing particularly in the fields of science and technology,
have all helped to hasten the arrival of mechanised indexing.
In a way, the principles on which mechanised indexing have
been developed are nothing new since they depend to a large
extent on titles and wording that accurately convey the true
meaning of the text they are trying to describe. Thus they are
exploiting the implications of the author's title or the abstrac-
tor's summary through their actual words and, to this extent,
they are following out the keyword or Schlagwort system once
used more haphazardly by Poole and his contemporaries (see
page 18). This method is being used nowadays with particular
success in the indexing of titles of scientific and technical articles
in periodicals, where the exactness of language is in noticeable
contrast to the more fanciful titles used in works relating to the
humanities.

An interesting example of the mechanised systems now in use
can be cited from the recent files of the *Bioresearch Index* (Bio-
sciences Information Service of *Biological Abstracts*, Philadelphia).
This remarkable publication indexes in several different ways
the contents of a large number of English and foreign-language
journals in its field. Included in the April 1968 (No. 4) issue of
this index is a reference to an article by A. J. Kukushkin and
A. N. Kuznetsov which appeared on pages 253 to 258 of issue No.
11 (2) of the 1966 volume of *Biophysics* with the following title:

Possible physical mechanisms of thermo luminescence of
certain aromatic amino-acids and proteins

To the title of this article *Bioresearch Index* assigned the serial number 25463, thus providing it with a unique reference as far as this particular indexing service is concerned.

To exploit to the full the very specific title of such an article, and thus enable it to be found by searchers who only remember part of the title or, being unaware of its existence, are checking instead for any recent material on a certain aspect, the computer is programmed to index the title by all its *significant* words. To do this, it permutates the title in a systematic way that can perhaps best be visualised by imagining the title's being written on a band or ring:

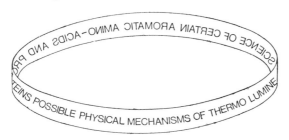

If one imagines this band revolving, but halting momentarily each time a complete word comes before the lens of a camera so that the whole visible text can be photographed, it will be seen that on the front of the band some words will precede the word in question, while others will follow it—in either case, what is visible may include at either end some incomplete words, as in the illustration above.

The line of type in the index, in common with most such systems, allows room for only a limited number of characters (usually eighty) including spaces between words so that, unless a title is very short, it is unlikely that the full effective wording will ever appear in any of the index entries. Nevertheless, sufficient is shown within the space available for the searcher to be able to gain a general idea of the subject content of the article, together with the all-essential serial reference number. In the present case, the *Bioresearch Index* did not index every word in the title, but in its Subject Index it made entries for amino-acids, aromatic amino-acids, luminescence, mechanisms, physical mechanisms, proteins, and thermo luminescence—thus covering all *significant* words in the following way:

(1)	(2)	(3)
NCE OF CERTAIN AROMATIC	AMINO-ACIDS AND PROTEINS/ POSSIBLE P	25463
LUMINESCENCE OF CERTAIN	AROMATIC AMINO-ACIDS AND PROTEINS/ P	25463
AL MECHANISMS OF THERMO	LUMINESCENCE OF CERTAIN AROMATIC AMI	25463
EINS/ POSSIBLE PHYSICAL	MECHANISMS OF THERMO LUMINESCENCE OF	25463
AND PROTEINS/ POSSIBLE	PHYSICAL MECHANISMS OF THERMO LUMINE	25463
ROMATIC AMINO-ACIDS AND	PROTEINS/ POSSIBLE PHYSICAL MECHANIS	25463
PHYSICAL MECHANISMS OF	THERMO LUMINESCENCE OF CERTAIN AROMA	25463

In the printed index these entries are of course interspersed with thousands of others in the alphabetical sequence and therefore appear at great distances from each other. It will be noted that the central column (2) is the all-essential one, since this column determines the position of each entry in the overall alphabet while, for this purpose column (1) is irrelevant and, in the case of *Bioresearch Index* is therefore ingeniously shaded so that it tends to take a secondary place—an innovation that would be welcome in all indexes of this kind. It will be noticed that the front on the band in the illustration on page 151 shows the wording of line 4.

There are several points to note. As it is essential to show clearly where the title ends, this is indicated by inserting an oblique stroke followed by a space. In the fifth and seventh lines the beginning of the wording in column (1) is indented one space, the reason being that each of these lines starts with a complete word and therefore—by the nature of the computer's present method of working—they must include a space before the first word (a similar effect would be found at the end of any line in columns (1) or (2) where a word was completed one space from the end of the line). And, in each line the specific number reference is given in column (3): only by providing this numerical reference can the searcher be directed to the contents lists of journals in which the name of the journal, its specific issue and date of publication, and the complete title of the article and the names of its authors can be discovered. The entry in this case reads:

BIOPHYSICS

11 (2).   1966

25463   KUKUSHKIN A J   KUZNETSOV A N

POSSIBLE PHYSICAL MECHANISMS OF

THERMO LUMINESCENCE OF CERTAIN

AROMATIC AMINO-ACIDS AND PROTEINS/

PAGE 253–258

This entry, which appears in the first section of *Bioresearch Index* is in fact the all-important one for it is the only entry that includes all the essential details and it is from this information that all the successive indexes are mechanically prepared by the computer—not only the Subject Index which has been described above, but also the Author Index, and the Co-ordinate Indexes as well. Thus the searcher has every chance of discovering what he requires: he may simply be checking to ascertain whether any recent material has been published on amino-acids, proteins, thermo luminescence, etc.; he may half remember the article in question and be trying to identify it from one or two half-remembered words; he may be checking what work has recently been published by Kukushkin or Kuznetsov; or, he may be trying to find out if any work is being done on thermo luminescence in connection with proteins, etc. Whatever his approach, therefore, he stands a very good chance of finding what he requires quickly and, moreover, of not missing any important development in his field.

Several restrictions will have been noticed. In the entries above all the information is printed in capitals—not the easiest form for quick reading. The computer designers have now overcome this difficulty and it seems probable that all-capitals entries will shortly be a thing of the past. Secondly, in the body of the entry, mathematical and other symbols, Greek and other non-roman letters, etc., must be spelt out if they are to be included. Thus $\Delta\beta\gamma$ would, for this purpose, be expanded to:

DELTA BETA GAMMA

thus taking up over five times the space of the original letters. In the third place, a line of eighty characters is of course not nearly enough for any but indicative purposes and so small a line exerts an artificial restraint on the possibilities of computer indexing and gives a bewildering impression to those who are not familiar with this form of analysing information. Here again the computer designers have made a breakthrough and restriction to one-line entries is no longer essential and may soon also disappear with so many more teething troubles.

The system of indexing described here is known as KWIC (*keyword in context*) indexing, which was first developed by IBM. As can readily be appreciated, its success depends entirely on the degree of accuracy with which the title conveys the subject approach of the material being indexed. Thus it will continue to have greater advantages for scientific and technical matters than for items relating to literary or artistic fields where a title may often be an allusion to a central theme, based on a literary reference that can either be relied upon to evoke a response in the reader from his general cultural background, or which is explained at some point in the text (e.g. Mr. W. H. Auden's article 'The Idle Word, The Black Word'—*ALA Bulletin*, April 1968, pp. 403–406). Therefore, if this form of mechanised indexing is to be extended to all forms of publications, greater co-operation than has hitherto existed will be essential between author and indexer. In the case of an allusive title, it will be necessary to add a factual title or an accurate summary of the article so that it can be correctly indexed by the computer. Moreover, it will sooner or later be essential for such a title or summary to be written in terms based on a common and somewhat restricted thesaurus so that each word is unambiguous and conveys only one meaning as far as the computer is concerned. This is especially important in the case of the KWOC (*keyword out of context*) system in which index entries are sometimes compiled without the aid of supporting information (such as the words immediately before and immediately after the word indexed), so that words that have several different meanings—a very large number in the vocabulary of most languages—are either defined or are eliminated from the computer's thesaurus.

The indexer, having weighed up all these considerations, will see that the impact of the machine is not to be feared but rather to be welcomed. Whatever the machine can do, it still needs and will always need the expert help of the indexer to iron out the problems of complex indexing, to produce the finished product from the computer's raw material, and to plan the great advances that yet lie well ahead of present-day mechanised indexing.

Note: Readers who would like to pursue this fascinating subject in greater detail are recommended to study:

National Federation of Science Abstracting and Indexing Services, Annual Meeting, Philadelphia, March 1967 MAMMAX: MAchine-Made and MAchine Aided IndeX. Edited by S. Juhasz. San Antonio, Texas, Southwest Research Institute, Applied Mechanics Reviews, 1968 (AMR Report, no. 45).

This fully describes and illustrates the mechanised information services provided by eighteen leading American institutions: the Atomic Energy Commission (AEC), the American Society for Testing and Materials (ASTM), Chemical Abstract Service (CAS), the Defense Documentation Center (DDC), the National Aeronautics and Space Administration (NASA), the National Library of Medicine (NLM), Psychological Abstracts (PA), etc. It is particularly valuable for its examples of such systems as KWIC, KWOC, and many other methods which—when referred to by the abbreviations only—can puzzle the reader who is not in touch with the very latest advances.

Mechanised indexing

The chief expense involved in establishing a punched-card file is not the cost of the cards or the cost of the operations of putting the information on the cards; it is in obtaining the information to go on the cards, involving as it does literature searching and coding which must be done by a technically trained person.
S. C. STANFORD and C. D. GULL:
Transcription problems in preparing and using punched-card files

IF ONLY THERE WERE A MACHINE to do all this!' must have been murmured by thousands of indexers in the past as they tackled the more mechanical and boring parts of their tasks. Today the application of machines to the routine aspects of indexing has already begun and, in a few cases, has reached a high degree of efficiency. In the most advanced cases mechanisation of indexing has only been achieved by the use of expensive machines requiring the services of a relatively large number of staff, so that their employment is solely justified by the vast nature of the tasks to be undertaken, and by the speedier and more detailed results which they can obtain. This need not deter the average indexer from at least considering what measure of mechanisation lies within his grasp, and what more—with the coming of mass-produced equipment—may shortly be at his disposal.

Developments up to the present time have mainly been made possible by the adaptation of business machines which were designed specifically for large-scale accountancy and statistical work. The limitations of these machines for indexing purposes lie largely in the fact that they have been adapted rather than designed for indexing, and thus the future possibilities of mechanical indexing may be infinitely greater once inventors and designers have in mind the individual problems of indexers. In the main, present developments concern the uses of various forms of punched cards and electronic equipment, though microphotographic techniques are already beginning to play their part, so that the future indexing machine may well be one which combines the most useful features of all three.

One of the simplest types of mechanisation is an inexpensive system which any indexer may use without difficulty and which he will find of great assistance in those most tedious operations: sorting and resorting. The only equipment needed is a batch of marginally-punched cards, a small clipper and a knitting-needle of slightly smaller diameter than the holes in the cards. Using 5 in. by 3 in. or 8 in. by 5 in. marginally-punched cards, on which there may be as many as one hundred holes, the indexer can assign the holes to a variety of purposes. For example, the top row of holes can be allotted to the different letters of the alphabet, while the lower row can be divided up according to every ten pages of the book to be indexed. The actual process of indexing then continues in the ordinary way with the system of making each index entry on a separate card. When the indexer has written his entry he clips the appropriate marginal-positions on the card to correspond with the first letter of the entry and the tens figure of the page reference.

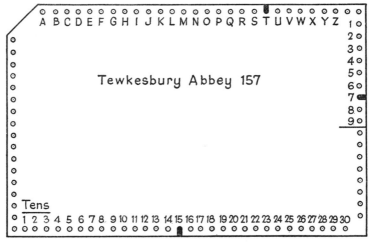

Here the letter T has been clipped for the initial letter of Tewkesbury, and the figure 15 has been clipped for the tens position of 157. By allocating ten holes, for the figures 0 to 9, on one of the side sequences of holes, it will also be possible to make the sorting by numbers more accurate still since the whole number of the page reference will be available with only one additional sorting. Thus, in the illustration above, the figure 7 of the page reference 157 has been punched in the right-hand margin. The holes still unused can be utilised for second letters, for special points such as the name and date of a periodical, or for mathematical or other symbols. In the illustration the numbers and letters are actually shown, but there is no need for the card itself to be marked in this way. Use of a transparent master-card of such a material as Perspex marked with the appropriate divisions will overcome the delay and expense of indicating the actual divisions on every card. It will be noticed that the top left-hand corner has been cut diagonally; this is to ensure that in sorting no card is filed upside down or back to front.

With practice the clipping of the cards presents no difficulties or undue delay. There is no need to sort the cards in any way until the stage is reached where it is essential to have them in one alphabetical or numerical order. Thus, when the indexing is completed—or at any time beforehand—the cards are ready for preliminary sorting. Taking a batch of cards—not more than two hundred at a time—and fanning them out slightly, the indexer thrusts the knitting needle through the hole denoting the letter A and shakes the cards, on which the index entries beginning with A will fall out. This process is repeated batch by batch and letter by letter until, at the end all the cards will be found to have been sorted automatically into the order of the letters of the alphabet. With regard to numerical sorting by page references, the cards are first sorted by tens—i.e. the lower row of holes—and then each set of tens can be sorted into exact order by using the right-hand row of holes (if the pattern of the illustration above is followed). Similarly, sorting by second letters of the alphabet can be achieved by allocating another set of 26 holes to an additional alphabet, so that the final sorting into exact alphabetical order will have been reduced to very small proportions and the labour of handling great masses of cards largely eliminated. Thus not only is the remainder of the sorting more easily carried out since only small batches of cards have to be handled at one time, but even space requirements for sorting are less and a small sorting board can take the place of a dining table or a work bench.

When the typing of the index has been completed from the cards in alphabetical order, the cards can be resorted in numerical order in much less time since each hole at the foot of the card represents only ten divisions as against the twenty-six of the alphabetical divisions. The ability to sort and resort cards in this fashion is of great encouragement to the indexer who, feeling his burden substantially reduced, can concentrate on the more intellectual aspects of his task.

With a little ingenuity the marginal holes can be made to achieve very much more for the indexer by making use of a series of shorthand methods based on well-known mathematical facts. Thus, while it is tempting to allocate the twenty-six holes at the top of the card to the different letters of the alphabet, this will only enable the indexer to sort by initial letters, whereas the same number of holes can be used for the first *four* letters in each word:

1 2 3 4 5 6	1 2 3 4 5 6	1 2 3 4 5 6	1 2 3 4 5 6	
o o o o o o	o o o o o o	o o o o o o	o o o o o o	o o
Initial letter	Second letter	Third letter	Fourth letter	Special

In this pattern each letter is punched by a code:

Letter	Position(s) to be punched	Letter	Position(s) to be punched
A	1	L	1 and 6
B	2	M	2 and 3
C	3	N	2 and 4
D	4	O	2 and 5
E	5	P	2 and 6
F	6	Q	2 and 6
G	1 and 2	R	3 and 4
H	1 and 3	S	3 and 5
I	1 and 4	T	3 and 6
J	1 and 4	U	4 and 5
K	1 and 5	V	4 and 5
		W	4 and 6
		X, Y, Z	5 and 6

N.B. The 'Special' divisions can be used for foreign letters, mathematical symbols, etc.

Thus in the example TEWKESBURY ABBEY, letter T is entered in the Initial letter division by punching holes 3 and 6, and letter E is entered in the Second letter division by punching hole 5, W is punched in the Third letter division at holes 4 and 6, and K in the Fourth letter division by punching holes 1 and 5:

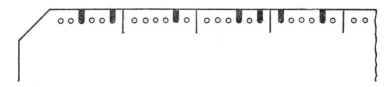

It will be noticed that the groups of letters P and Q, U and V, and X, Y, and Z, have each been given only one set of punching symbols: this enables the number of holes allocated to the alphabet to be limited to six and will not impede sorting to any great extent, though some hand sorting of these particular groups will of course be necessary. It will also be noticed that it has been possible to punch the first four letters of Tewkesbury Abbey with only seven punchings: an economy which confirms that punched cards can materially aid the indexer.

Similarly, figures can be handled expeditiously:

a b c d	a b c d	a b c d	a b c d	a b c d		
o o o o	o o o o	o o o o	o o o o	o o o o	o o o o	o o
units	tens	hundreds	thousands	ten thousands	hundred thousands	millions

In this case the code is even simpler since there are fewer divisions to be handled:

Number	Position(s) to be punched	Number	Position(s) to be punched
0	a	6	a and d
1	b	7	b and c
2	c	8	b and d
3	d	9	c and d
4	a and b		
5	a and c		

So that in the page reference 157 to Tewkesbury Abbey, the figure 7 would be punched in the units division by clipping

L

holes b and c, the figure 5 would be punched in the Tens division by clipping holes a and c, and then figure 1 would be clipped in the Hundreds division at hole b:

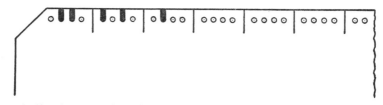

and clipping numbers in this fashion will be sufficient to achieve complete mechanical sorting for page references in books even up to encyclopaedia level, while the alphabetical system can bring about preliminary sorting to at least the fourth letter and —by using additional holes on the sides—even more detailed indexing. The codes must of course be used for sorting, but they are both so simple that those who use them constantly will find that they quickly memorise the symbols for the more frequently used letters and numbers.

Even so, the indexer who is attracted to punched cards as a means of solving some of his difficulties, is still on the threshold of their full resources. In the first place it is possible to double (at the very least) the amount of mechanical subdivision by having double rows of holes on the margins—even triple rows are sometimes used, but the technique at this point begins to become burdensome for the average person. Secondly, there are the remarkable possibilities of internally-punched cards. It is usually assumed the internally-punched cards need machines for their handling, but there is at least one variety which requires nothing more than the simplest of punching devices plus a keen eye. The credit for this is due to an Englishman, though both the French and the Americans were not far behind in discovering the same principle. More than twenty-five years ago Dr. W. E. Batten, in investigating the field of current patents in plastic technology for Imperial Chemical Industries, developed a system of indexing whose ingenuity is only matched by the simplicity of its operation. Briefly, if the same position is accurately punched on two or more cards and those cards are then held up to the light in register, it will be possible to see a shaft of light through those holes. Now, if each card is made to represent a subject and each hole the number of a document, the applications to large-scale periodical or office indexing become apparent.

For example, a lawyer who wishes to maintain an index of all the items relating to various people with whom he has business dealings may make cards for each of these people. Assuming that Messrs. Brown & Co. are mentioned in letter number 126 as defendants in a case involving Messrs. Jones & Co., and in letter number 179 as agents for the Ocean Liner Co., the card for this firm will be punched accordingly:

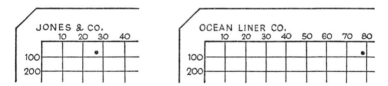

Similarly the cards for the Ocean Liner Co. and Messrs. Jones will be punched in the appropriate positions:

Thus, if all the documents relating to Messrs. Brown & Co. are needed it is simply necessary to read off the numbers of the documents punched on that firm's card. If, on the other hand, the document concerning Messrs. Brown's dealings with the Ocean Liner Co. is required, all that is necessary is to place together the cards relating to the two firms and to read off the number(s) where a pinpoint of light shines through the two cards. (The connection with co-ordinate indexing will be obvious to readers of pages 144–49). When Dr. Batten first invented this system he used a card 8 in. by 10 in. with 400 positions for punching. Later he used a Hollerith card with 800 punching positions. Then an American firm invented a card 8 in. by 6 in. with a simple manual punching device which enables no less than 18,000 distinct punchings to be made on a single face. This type of card would cover the requirements of most small offices that would rarely want to keep more than this number of documents in current use, while for larger concerns provision may be easily made by providing extra cards of different colours for further sequences. Thus a five-card system would cover 90,000 documents and yet take up very little room and cost very little.

The use of this form of punched card for book-indexing is slight, apart from the detailed analysis of encyclopaedias and very large composite reference works, but there are many possibilities with regard to periodical indexing. For example, in a magazine on Yachting it may sometimes be desirable to refer to articles on the building of a yacht, at other times to its performance in various races and at still others to its owners. Similarly, the approach may at other times be from the point of view of yacht builders, particular anchorages, etc. Here the resources of the Batten (or, to give it its American title: Peek-a-Boo) system are inestimable. Nevertheless, it remains an office indexing system, as distinct from printed indexes, though it may always be used as a basis for the latter.

Research

*Let me hear no more of him, Sir. That is
the fellow who made the Index to my
RAMBLERS, and set down the name of
Milton thus: Milton, Mr. John.*
SAMUEL JOHNSON (1709–84)

THE INCREASING USE of the computer in everyday life was
bound to encourage investigation of its application to indexing,
and much of the resulting effort has been devoted to eliminating
the human element. It is therefore heartening to find Professor
Harold Borko saying as recently as 1970 that 'the computer can
be used as an aid in book indexing, but indexing is still not a
fully automatic process.' He adds: 'Machine indexing is also
expensive and thus not a substitute for human indexing.' It
would be wrong however to underestimate the degree of success
which research in this field has already achieved, just as it
would be a pity to remain unaware of the ingenuity and re-
source shown by research workers in the area of automated
indexing.

Professor Borko's remarks apply only to book indexing. The
main research effort covers a far wider territory and is particularly addressed to the analysis of unpublished reports, the contents of periodicals, the texts of the proceedings of conferences,
and similar materials. Moreover, research is not limited to the
indexing of information. Commendably it pays as much attention to the needs of the users of indexes, and to their degree of
success in obtaining information through indexes. Until recently
this has been an aspect which has been almost wholly neglected:
whatever research is now carried out cannot but help the indexers of the future to provide more useful indexes.

To return, for a moment, to book indexes. The average book
comprises a large amount of knowledge and ideas already
generally known and accepted, to which is added a small

quantity of new and original knowledge and ideas. It is conceivable therefore that the indexes in existing works on the same subject could form a good basis for constructing indexes to later contributions. Thus, some research has already been done in making book indexes by forming a group of index headings from works published in a given subject field and feeding these into a computer. If a paper tape is then made of the text of a new book at the same time as it is being typed, the tape text can be compared with the list of subject headings held in the computer, and an acceptable index to most of its contents will be forthcoming—indeed, in the case of a new textbook, the index thus produced may cover the entire contents, if the text only includes well-established facts and ideas. It then only remains for the indexer to edit the index, add entries for new names, new concepts, etc., not included in the computerised list of headings, and to ensure that the page references are inserted in due course.

The advantages of such a system could never be more than marginally financial; they are more likely to include speed of preparation, and evenness and comprehensiveness of treatment. The latter point is one that most concerns indexers, for few would deny that the quality of human indexing is very vulnerable to fatigue, inattention, and—over a lengthy period—inequality of treatment. On the other hand, the automatic treatment by computer of the great bulk of the indexing task, can enable the indexer to produce a work of very high quality, and the progress of research on these lines brings closer to the present the day when the indexer will be handed, together with the proofs of a book, a rough computerised index as a basis on which to build his final work.

Research into large-scale indexing of the vast range of current information—especially in the fields of science and technology—has taken many forms, but it is almost always based on recognition of the necessity for matching the initial indexing with the eventual lines of approach of the users of the index. Unlike book indexing, research in this area concentrates on matching the overall content of a document with a group of subject headings, rather than indexing it sentence by sentence. Since these groups of headings may range from two or three to as many as forty or fifty per document it could be argued that

it is difficult to discern any real difference between the two processes. It does however exist for, if a book is included among the
other types of documents being indexed, the entries for that
book will in effect represent the general content of the individual
chapters rather than an analysis of those chapters sentence by
sentence.

Research in this area almost always assumes for experimental
purposes that the complete text of a document—or, at the very
least, a thorough abstract of its contents—can initially be fed
into a computer, so that various automated systems can be
studied in an attempt to discover how far they can achieve
satisfactory indexing of that document. One system is the word-
count, by which the text can be analysed into its constituent
words. It is clear that if a document uses such words as 'war',
'guns', 'armaments', 'ammunition', etc., a very great number
of times, then index entries made under these headings are
likely to enable a great majority of the people interested in
those subjects find something useful to them.

It can be seen that such a system could have a high degree
of success with names of people and places, and with subjects
and ideas that can be represented by single words. Where it
would fail would be in the more sophisticated areas. For example, in the case of 'solid state physics', 'black box', 'silent
majority', 'credibility gap', or 'police state', the phrases represent much more than the sum of the meanings of their constituent words. With this in mind, research into automated
indexing has therefore paid particular attention to the problem
of word-combinations, for there is the added complication that,
e.g., while the expression 'black box' may occur in many places
in the text, both 'black 'and 'box' may also occur separately in
other contexts.

The contiguity of words in specific contexts is therefore of the
highest importance, and the computer is accordingly programmed to take special care of the multi-word concept,
though this will still not cope with casual couplings such as
'peripheral journals' or 'minor politicians' which may have
undertones in their own context. Since the viewpoint of the
eventual user is however being kept firmly in mind, this is less of
a problem than it might at first appear to be. For the enquirer
a thesaurus or list of subject-headings actually in use is main-

tained. In controlled experiments volunteers are asked to choose subject-headings—or groups of subject-headings—which they believe may represent fields of knowledge that particularly interest them. By programming these on a computer, the original documents they represent are brought to light. The volunteers can then examine them and determine how closely they reflect their interests. A repetition of this experiment, taking into account the adjustments instigated by the volunteers' comments, helps to make the indexing system more precise and useful.

This in turn brings up two aspects on which much research effort has been expended: 'recall' and 'precision'. For example, if from a collection of one thousand documents on English literature it is necessary to produce all those with any important contribution on Milton, it would be possible to obtain 100 per cent 'recall' by handing over *all* the documents since, in this way, it would be certain that nothing had been overlooked. Assuming however that the collection includes only fifty documents with any important contribution on Milton, the 'precision' percentage would only be five, for it would be necessary to look through twenty documents to find one relevant item. On the other hand, if only the thirty documents whose titles definitely indicate they deal with Milton are handed over, it is clear that twenty more have been overlooked and, while the 'recall' will be 60 per cent (i.e. thirty out of fifty documents), the 'precision' rate will be 100 per cent, since all the documents produced are relevant.

In automated indexing, both those factors have their uses. A company considering the launching of a new product will first of all want to make a general survey of the market to discover whether such a project is at all feasible. For this purpose a few well-selected relevant documents will suffice to ensure that the company is adequately informed of the main aspects involved. Here is a case where total 'recall' is unnecessary, but where 'precision' is of great importance. Once having decided that the idea is worth pursuing, the company then authorises a very thorough investigation of the whole project, and is therefore interested in making certain of seeing every piece of information on the subject, no matter how much irrelevant material is combed in the process. At this stage 'precision' is less important than total 'recall', for the omission of even an obscure item might produce difficulties for the company at a later period. It is important however to bear in mind that in any indexing service, the nearer total 'recall' of relevant documents is approached, the lower will be the degree of 'precision' and vice versa.

Whatever system is used in producing documents for research workers, a certain amount of 'noise' will be generated—that is, they will be offered documents which are not relevant to their interests. This can arise in many ways. For example, if the research worker is interested in processes for manufacturing improved plastic containers for magnetic tapes, special care must be taken if—along with articles and reports on this subject—others are not included on plastic tapes and on magnetic containers. To counter this type of problem, a number of ingenious devices have been tried out, notably 'links' and 'rôles'. Thus, in this example, the programming of the computer would include the instructions that 'containers' must be linked with 'plastic' and 'tapes' with 'magnetic', and that the 'rôle' of the 'plastic containers' in enclosing the 'magnetic tapes' must be observed. To ensure such points, the 'links' and 'rôles' are coded in the initial indexing of the documents. The drawback here is the complexity of the indexing process and the difficulty of defining the functions or properties of the index entries, and recently there has been a tendency to retreat from overmuch attention to defining 'links' and 'rôles', though their use within a very limited and well-documented subject-field can be very valuable.

Another interesting line of research deals with the incidence of several of the same groups ('clumps') of terms appearing in different documents. Such 'clumping' becomes apparent in any computer analysis of the text, and is seen to be strong evidence of similar subject coverage—either complete or overlapping— of these documents. Once this characteristic has been recognised, it is a logical step to search for similar 'clumps' in other documents, thereby strengthening the indexing process and making additional relevant items available to users.

Research from the users' standpoint has steadily progressed. It is no new development in libraries for readers to be asked to be kept informed of the acquisition of new items that may particularly interest them. It was however H. P. Luhn who recognised that in today's situation of millions of documents, this service to users should be put on a more scientific basis. His 'SDI' (*S*elective *D*issemination of *I*nformation) system was based on the need for building an individual 'profile' of each user's specific interests, and for keeping that 'profile' up-to-date as those interests changed. The profiles nowadays are usually couched in the same terms as are used in the index to the documents to which the users have access, and as these terms are listed, defined and cross-referenced in a 'thesaurus', the profiles have a very good chance of being 'matched' by relevant new documents as they are received. The matching is of course done by computer. By means of simple questionnaires, attached to the documents sent to enquirers, it is possible to assess the degree of service this system is achieving at any given time—and this also helps in the adjustment of the profiles when the user has failed to notify his change of interests.

One of the most fascinating developments in automated indexing is the rapid growth of 'citation indexing'. This, in itself, is no new concept, for it has an honorable and long history in the legal field where lawyers for many years past have been citing past precedents in support of their argument. It remained however to be exploited in other subject areas when Dr. Eugene Garfield pointed out that in the scientific field research workers usually quoted the work of their predecessors, and therefore new indexing procedures could be developed from this custom. Dr. Garfield showed that by appropriate indexing it would be possible to pursue a topic on which a significant paper had been issued, by studying the works in which it was later cited.

Thus, if Dupré in France wrote an important paper on a new strain of plant bacteria which, unknown to him, Jones in England was also investigating, the interests of both would come to light a little later when Takimoto in Japan cited the work of both in a paper that took the experiments a stage further. Citation indexing can therefore produce automatically something that conventional automated indexing only imperfectly achieves, since—without the trouble of working out new and adequate subject-headings—the whole field of contributions on a subject will come to light providing each research worker cites the writings of his predecessors and colleagues. In science, moreover, the effective life of a scientific paper is usually no more than five years, so that citation indexes are not likely to become unduly inflated.

To the basic citation index, comprising the author and title of each original paper plus references to all subsequent papers in which it is cited, has now been added a number of adjuncts, enabling users to exploit this tool still more thoroughly. Anyone, scientist or no, examining the current issues of the *Science citation index*, will recognise what a remarkable step forward has been made in current indexing techniques. A particular use of this index may be used in pursuing the subject of this chapter, since the writings of most of the outstanding research workers in the field of indexing are included there.

These include Professor Harold Borko's very frank and stimulating article on 'Experiments in book indexing by computer' (*Information storage and retrieval*, volume 6, 1970, pages 5–16) from which the quotations in the first paragraph of this chapter have been taken; and his *Automated language processing* (New York, Wiley, 1967) remains the standard work on the subject. M. E. Stevens's *Automatic indexing: a state of the art report* (Washingon, D.C., National Bureau of Standards, 1965. NBS Monograph no. 91) is still the best survey of the whole field. For the 1971 Annual Conference of the National Federation of Scientific Abstracting and Indexing Services, Dr. Stephen Juhasz was asked to organise a session on indexing: one of the results was an extraordinarily detailed and fascinating report called *Cinderella: author index practices and philosophies* (San Antonio, Texas, Applied Mechanics Reviews, 1971. AMR Report no. 54), which covers the author indexing methods of nineteen organisations. Especially interesting are its discussions of problems such as name versus person indexing, manual versus computer filing, transliteration, finding proper surnames, the lack of cost-effectiveness data, and the utility of author indexes versus subject indexes.

Another well-known research worker in this field is Professor C. D. Batty whose 'The automatic generation of index languages' (*Journal of documentation*, volume 25, no. 2, June 1969, pages 142–51) summarises recent attempts to generate index languages by the statistical analysis of text. On the 'clumping' theory two papers by A. F. Parker-Rhodes have been issued by the Cambridge Language Research Unit: *The theory of clumps* (1960), and *Contributions to the theory of clumps* (1961). Susan Artandi's *An introduction to computers in information science* (Metuchen, N.J., Scarecrow Press, 1968) is an excellent guide to some of the most interesting aspects of automated indexing.

It would be impossible to read widely in this area without coming across numerous references to the Aslib Cranfield Project, which has been examining and comparing in depth the performance of various indexing systems in use today. The best account of this important enquiry is Cyril W. Cleverdon's basic work *Factors determining the performance of indexing systems* (Cranfield, College of Aeronautics, 1966. 2 volumes), supplemented by the Project's later reports. Information on what is being done elsewhere is given in M. Coyaud's *L'Analyse automatique des documents* (Paris, Mouton, 1967). Luhn's SDI theory is described in his 'Selective dissemination of the new scientific information' (*American documentation*, volume 12, 1961, pages 131 onwards).

Many of these contributions to present-day research in indexing are written in somewhat technical language. For more easily assimilable summaries of the present state of the art, the reader is recommended to study the relevant articles in the new *Encyclopedia of library and information science* (New York, Dekker, 1968 to date), of which the first six volumes have been issued so far. Notable among these are 'Aspect systems' by Joshua Stern (volume 1, pages 669–71); 'Chain indexing' by Professor Batty (volume 4, pages 423–34); and the following articles in volume 5: 'Citation indexes' by Melvin Weinstock (pages 16–40), the 'Theory of clumps' by Karen Sparck Jones (pages 208–24), 'Computers and computing' by Jack Belzer and James Williams (pages 538–84), 'Concordances' by Roberto Busa (pages 592–604), the 'Conference on Information Retrieval and Machine Translation' by Allen Kent (pages 604–606), 'Concept coordination' by Fred Whaley (pages 584–86), and 'Coordinate indexing' by Susan Artandi (pages 679–82). The bibliographies appended to these articles are well selected and will lead the reader to the chief sources on each subject.

Conclusion

Few authors, I suspect, are temperament-
ally capable of making their own index.
ALEC CLIFTON-TAYLOR: An Open
Letter to a Publisher

THE BEST WAY TO BEGIN to learn the art of indexing is to study
existing indexes and to make extensive use of them. None
knows better than the research worker, as he looks for his
material, what the ideal index should be. Every failure to find
an important item emphasises the point that an index must
provide the reader with the material he wants, no matter what
logical heading he looks under. Every omission underlines the
necessity for indexing everything, for no one can judge what
may be of importance in the future. Every misprint and wrong
entry brings home the point that accuracy is essential.

As the research worker proceeds, he finds to his dismay that
indexes vary a great deal in their methods. There are first of
all the differences in alphabetisation. To the experienced reader
this presents no great difficulty, for he perceives almost immediately and instinctively what method is in force, but nevertheless there is the possibility of missing items which increases
with the degree of inexperience of the searcher. Then there are
the different systems of sub-arrangement under the main headings, and the various ways of setting them out in type. Even
the references may be given in different ways: some to pages,
some to parts of pages, and others to paragraphs. Some indexes
will enter under the popular forms of names and subjects, others
under scientific equivalents. Each index and its methods, in fact,
must be studied individually if the utmost is to be obtained
from it, and this may mean reading ill-written and imperfect
instructions or, worse still, finding none and working out the
rules for oneself by which the indexer has made his compilation.
This is worth doing for a book which is likely to be often used,

but it is time-wasting and annoying to have to do it for only one or two references.

Newspaper indexes can be very difficult: the old index to *The Times*—*Palmer's Index*—valuable though it is, is one of the most difficult to use. While deaths, for instance, are entered under that word, performances of plays appear under Theatres. *The Times Official Index* is itself an individual affair whose methods must be very carefully studied: here deaths are entered individually, and performances of plays under Theatrical productions. The test with such indexes is to try to study the continuation of a news story which carries on beyond the turn of the year (and thus, into a new volume of the index). Certainly any research worker who is likely to carry out extensive work on news indexes should practise for a time before embarking on his investigations. This practice is especially important in the case of the indexes to government publications, for here the possibility of missing items is only too real. In fact, the indexes to this important class of publications are very difficult to use, and would benefit from a more scientific method of compilation. For instance, in the February, 1951, *Government Publications Monthly List*, Cmd. Paper No. 8153, which is the *North of Scotland Hydro-Electric Board Constructional Scheme No. 56: Stornaway Generating Station*, has no index entry under Stornaway, while the Ministry of Supply's *Specifications, D.T.D.*, are not indexed individually at all.

The study of the best kinds of indexes will improve the skill of the indexer. One of the finest indexes is that to the *Encyclopaedia Britannica*: here every important item is analytically indexed, and no matter what heading the reader looks under, there is a very good hope of finding what he wants. Another very good index will be found in the new edition of *Chambers's Encyclopaedia*, and the telephone directories and Kelly's directories are masterpieces of clear and careful indexing on a vast scale. But no matter what the book, the index should be examined and tested.

A good way of testing is to read a paragraph and then to try to discover under what headings it has been indexed. If it is easy to discover, then the indexing is good: if difficult, then the index is poor. A second method is to take index entries at random and then to turn to the pages referred to, and to see how well the index entries manage to suit the text matter. Tests such as these will soon rub in the requirements of a good index, and the types of references which are needed.

Some of the finest and greatest indexes are in the field of periodical indexing, and none is better than the great series of indexes issued by the H. W. Wilson Company of New York, except perhaps the independent *Public Affairs Information Service Bulletin*, which is compiled by a group of American librarians. The Wilson series include the *Reader's Guide to Periodical Literature* and the *Social Sciences and Humanities Index* (formerly the *International Index to Periodicals*), which are both general guides, and each cover many different periodicals. They are not only issued frequently and cumulated frequently throughout the year, but even their annual volumes are cumulated into three-yearly volumes so that reference to great groups of files of periodicals is particularly easy. In addition there are similar indexes to periodicals concerned with groups of subjects such as Agriculture, Art, Education, Applied Science and Technology, Essays and General Literature, etc.

The *Public Affairs Information Service Bulletin*, mentioned above, has a fine tradition of good indexing. The *Bulletin* covers both books and pamphlets, as well as periodical articles. Such indexes as these are not only worth studying: they can be used as models whose subject-headings can be used as a basis for one's own.

Few people will nowadays undertake indexing as a full-time job: the rewards are small and incommensurate with the amount of knowledge and experience required. Small wonder therefore that so many indexes are imperfectly compiled; like so many other things in life of importance to the community, they are scamped because few members of the public are aware of their importance, and few are willing to pay for them to be done properly.

Nevertheless, indexing has its interest, even its fascination for those who love knowledge and who are willing to devote some of their time to making it readily available to others. It is a task which is best carried out in an unhurried fashion, and yet which nearly always needs to be completed at high speed. Even so, there is no excuse for slipshod work: concentration and care will partly remedy the lack of time available.

It seems strange to speak of personality in connection with

indexing, and yet the personality of the indexer is never far behind the index. A careful study of any particular index will reveal something of the indexer's own outlook, especially in his selection and framing of descriptive subject-headings. In some indexes, too, there are more definite traces of personality, and some indexes can even be described as political, cynical, or even humorous.

There are many examples of humorous indexes, but one of the most outstanding is undoubtedly that which Sir Alan Herbert compiled to the volumes which comprise *Uncommon Law* (Methuen, 1935). This index is one of the few which can be said to be both interesting to read for itself, and also tantalising and provocative. Take, for example, the following extract:

MARRIAGE
    Admirals, denied benefits of, by inequitable treatment, 180
    Naval officers lured into, on false pretences, 180
    Not, legally, the same as slavery, 367
    Touching belief of Charlotte Watts in delights of, 144

In spite of the fantastic nature of the entries, reference to the actual pages shows that there is sound foundation for most of them. The effect is achieved by the application of a brilliant mind to a reputedly dull job, as may be seen in the following:

DRAINS
    need not be attended to, at the House of Commons, 421
EUROPA
    shocking allegations, 167
FISH-PORTERS
    said to suffer little hardship through high cost of libel actions, 56
Hamlet
    counts as a dog-race, 247
HIPPOPOTAMUS
    compared with Divorce Laws, 457
IMMORAL EARNINGS: *see* Post Office

The Hamlet entry, for instance, refers to the following passage: '"Entertainment" includes any exhibition, performance, amusement, game, or sport to which persons are admitted for payment, so that in the same wide category are included a performance of *Hamlet* and the racing of dogs, a religious drama and a travelling circus, the fiddling of a Kreisler and the roaring of a caged lion, a game of cricket or a tragedy of Ibsen.'

From this, it will be seen that the task of indexing need not be uninteresting, and that an index can not only be humorous, but even critical or tendentious, and that it can certainly be biased. In the past there have been several examples of books whose indexes, compiled by unscrupulous enemies, have been their ruin, and although some of the bad indexes of today are not quite as destructive, they certainly lessen the value of their books to many serious readers.

N.B. The American Society of Indexers was founded at the end of 1968. Details of membership may be obtained from the Secretary of the Society, Mrs. Marlene Hurst, University Microfilms, 300 North Zeed Road, Ann Arbor, Michigan 48106.

M

Further
reading

IF ONE BECOMES REALLY INTERESTED in a subject there is nearly always a desire to read more about it, and especially to study different views and methods. The literature of indexing unhappily is remarkably small. The first substantial work on the subject is Henry B. Wheatley's *What is an Index? a few Notes on Indexes and the Indexers.* 2nd edition. (Published for the Index Society by Longmans, Green, 1879.) Henry Wheatley was Honorary Secretary of the Index Society, which did so much work of a pioneer nature in the field, and which laid down the first set of sound rules for the compilation of indexes. The Society later changed its name to the British Records Association, and as such exists today. In this work, Wheatley provided a somewhat rambling but vastly entertaining account of the history of indexing, studded with anecdotes and apposite quotations. It formed the basis of his *How to make an Index* (Elliot Stock, 1902), which, in spite of its name is much more of a history than a practical manual. Its second chapter, on Amusing and Satirical Indexes, can especially be recommended. The Society of Indexers and The Library Association have commemorated his name in the Wheatley Medal, awarded annually to the maker of an outstanding index.

The more practical books came later. In 1921, George E. Brown published *Indexing: a Handbook of Instruction* (Grafton), a dry and somewhat dogmatic volume which describes methods of the author's unlikely to appeal to many indexers nowadays. A more helpful work is Archibald Leycester Clarke's *Manual of Practical Indexing, including Arrangement of Subject Catalogues* (Grafton) of which a second edition was published in 1933. Clarke's *Manual* deals more particularly with the indexing of works of the humanities, and devotes special chapters to the indexing of volumes of history and biography. A book which may be said to be complementary to it to a certain extent is John W. T. Walsh's *The Indexing of Books and Periodicals* (Arnold, 1930), for in this work much attention is paid to the indexing of scientific and technical books and periodicals, and many detailed examples are given.

But the finest manual on indexing is too little known: it is Marion Thorne Wheeler's *New York State Library Indexing: Principles, Rules and Examples*. 5th edition. (Albany, New York, University of the State of New York Press, 1957.) In spite of its uncompromisingly formal style and its undistinguished printing, this 78-page pamphlet covers every phase of indexing, and is full of good sensible advice and excellent examples of actual entries and of various kinds of indexes. A noteworthy feature of this work is its own index which, in just over five pages indexes the sixty-one pages of text in a thorough and workmanlike fashion.

Other helpful material includes ASLIB's *Report of Aslib Meeting on Indexing and Filing of Unpublished Material*, 15th February, 1946 (ASLIB, 1946), which describes the methods in use in commercial and research organisations, and includes an important contribution on filing policy and practice in the Civil Service (this latter was also printed in the *Journal of Documentation*, volume II, number 1). There are also many relevant items in the reports of the ASLIB Conferences, 1924 to date, obtainable from that Association. Recently an attractively produced pamphlet, M. D. Anderson's *Book Indexing* (Cambridge University Press, 1971), contributed a thirty-six-page informative essay summarising modern practice in a very readable fashion, and there is also Bertha M. Weeks's *Filing and Records Management* (3rd edition, New York, Ronald Press, 1964), which deals with the problems and methods of the modern office.

Even discussions of the philosophy and practice of indexing are few and far between: Sir Edward Cook's 'The Art of Indexing' in his *Literary Recreations* (Macmillan, 1918), gives a lively defence of the art of indexing, while E. B. Osborn contributes the lighter side in his 'Humours of Indexing' in his *Literature and Life* (New York, Dutton, 1922). R. L. Mégroz wrote three pages on 'What's in an index?' in *Thirty-one Bedside Essays* (Pen-in-

Hand, 1949), and the former librarian of the War Office, F. J. Hudleston, discusses both indexing and cataloguing in 'Librarians in Undress' in his *Warriors in Undress* (New York, Little, 1926). But the classic on indexing is Stephen Leacock's 'Index: there is no Index' in *My remarkable Uncle* (New York, Dodd, 1942), which has since been reprinted in several volumes, and from which the quotation on page 32 is taken.

Dr. J. Edwin Holmstrom in the 'Sorting and Interpreting of Facts and Ideas' in the second edition of his *Records and Research in Engineering and Industrial Science: a guide to the sources, processing and storekeeping of technical knowledge, with a chapter on translating* (Chapman & Hall, 1947), describes large-scale indexing such as is undertaken by great organisations, and explains the famous Kaiser system which was first introduced into this country some forty years ago by an American librarian. Dr. Holmstrom's pamphlet *How to Take, Keep and Use Notes* (ASLIB, 1947), describes a technique for storing items of information together with jottings of one's own ideas in such a way that any particular item can instantly be found when required, and every newly added item clarifies the picture in one's mind of what is already there.

One of the most fascinating books on the subject is John Lawler's *The H. W. Wilson Company* (New York, Columbia University Press, 1950), which is a racy and very readable account of the birth and development of the greatest indexing organisation of our times. In the course of explaining the remarkable career of this Company, Mr. Lawler conveys much interesting and useful information on modern methods of indexing. For computerised concordancing there is no better introduction than James Allan Painter's 'Programmer's Preface' in Stephen Maxfield Parrish's *A concordance to the poems of W. B. Yeats* (Cornell University Press, 1963, pages xxix–xxxvii).

In the wider field of book production, there is a handful of books which are not only helpful, but also make fascinating reading. Joseph Lasky's *Proofreading and Copy-preparation: a Textbook for the Graphic Arts Industry*. Second edition (New York, Mentor Press, 1954), is a mine of information on the intricacies of book making, although his treatment of indexing itself is too summary and arbitrary to content any but the casual enquirer. Another useful work is John Gloag's *How to Write Technical*

Books: with some Pertinent Remarks about Planning Technical Papers and Forms (Allen & Unwin, 1950), which covers all aspects of the making of books from the author's point-of-view, and contains some excellent remarks on index-construction on pages 120 to 124. But a book which is not only a pleasure to read, but also to handle and to own is *A Manual of Style: containing Typographical and other rules for Authors, Printers, and Publishers, recommended by the University of Chicago Press, together with Specimens of Type*, latest revised edition (Chicago, University of Chicago Press), which covers every phase of book making, includes many specimens of good modern types, and a glossary of technical terms. Its excellent chapter on *Indexes* is also available separately.

Another useful pamphlet in the excellent series—The Cambridge Authors' and Printers' Guides—to which Carey's essay also belongs, is Brooke Crutchley's *Preparation of Manuscripts and Correction of Proofs* (5th edition, Cambridge University Press, 1968). As the advertisement to this series stated: 'a good book in the reader's hand is always the result of collaboration between Author and Printer; that collaboration is closest when each knows just what help he can give or expect to receive.' The last recommendation is the 10th edition of F. Howard Collins' *Authors' and Printers' Dictionary* 10th edition, Oxford University Press, 1956), which gives authoritative rulings on so many points of spelling and other matters of writing for publication, that it is an essential part of any author or indexer's working library.

Three publications of the British Standards Institution are of outstanding inportance. *Recommendations for the preparation of indexes for books, periodicals and other publications* (BS 3700: 1964) is a 52-page guide to the content, construction, arrangement and preparation of indexes, outlining the basic indexing principles and practice. *Alphabetical arrangement* (BS 1749: 1968) is a set of rules designed to secure uniformity in the alphabetical arrangement of items in indexes, catalogues and lists of all kinds. *Bibliographical references* (BS1629: 1950, and Amendment PD 1186, May 1951) is an 18-page standard scheme for the preparation of references to literature, applying to entries for bibliographical lists and to particulars given for the identification of works referred to in reviews, abstracts, etc., but not necessarily applying to catalogues of particular collections. *Recommendations for proof correction and copy preparation* (BS 1219: 1958) will also be found to be an invaluable guide to correct practice. The U.S.A. Standards Institute published the revised edition of its *USA Standard for Indexes* in 1968.

The revised text of a series of lectures on the art of indexing given by a number of British experts, has been edited by one of the contributors, Mr. G. Norman Knight, under the title *Training in Indexing*, (Cambridge, Mass., M.I.T. Press, 1969).

In Part Three, an annotated list is given of the more important reference books which will help the indexer in the research which is part of his everyday work.

Part three

Reference
section

Schedule of
standard proof
correction marks

I know, too, how often an author, whether he knows it or not, was indebted to an indexer for pointing out errors, discrepancies, or repetitions that had otherwise escaped detection in the proofs.

THE RT. HON. HAROLD MACMILLAN

Caret or insertion mark. Repeat in margin and text.

Delete or take out matter crossed through (Greek theta on a stroke).

Close-up—probably misplaced space between letters.

Space sign. Instruction to add to spacing. If the contrary, prefix word 'less' to sign. Also eq. **#** mark strokes between words to be equally spaced.

Abbreviation for transpose. Mark all items to be moved. If more than two, advisable to number in correct order.

For transposition of letters in word. Mark 'trs.' in margin.

Underline matter to be italicised.

Change to roman; encircle affected words or letters.

Double underlining denotes small caps.

Triple underlining denotes caps.

Wavy underlining denotes bold face.

185

stet	Denote by dotted line below matter to be 'stetted'.
w.f.	Wrong fount. Mark through or encircle letter(s) incorrect.
≡	Straighten type. Repeat in margin and above and below affected matter.
≣	Diagonal strokes between lines of type to denote straightening required. Due to faulty locking up before proofing.
⁹⁄	Insert apostrophe. Always use caret mark in text to show insertion.
/-/	Insert hyphen.
⊢⊣	Insert dash.
⊙	Insert full stop.
⌐	See below (A).
⌐	See below (B).
⌐⌐	To move lines to right (i.e. to indent), note amount of movement in margin 1 em, etc. Mark same sign in text at left of matter to be moved. To move words in line use this sign textually and A above in margin.
⌐⌐	To move line to left, the converse of previous entry. Put textual markings at right of matter to be moved. For words in line use same sign, and B above in margin.
□	1 em. 1 en is half the width.
□□	2 ems, and so on.

| | Invert matter marked—usually single characters upside down. |

Broken letter. Stroke through character affected or encircle it.

Square brackets used to denote position required. Mark affected matter also at either end.

Run-on sign. Encircle matter to be run-on.

Raised space or letter.

Centre on line. Use to indicate position also.

This list is not exhaustive, but includes those marks generally in use, and the most likely to be necessary for correction of proofs.

It should be noted that it is advisable always to encircle or put a stroke through the affected letter(s) or word(s), whilst marking appropriate instructions in the margin(s). Such instructions should have a stroke between them and the text alongside in most, if not all, instances.

The chief requirement is to make all corrections legible. Should a marking be indeterminate, cross it through and repeat at side. Corrections are expensive, so avoid making a second proof correction necessary.

Corrections, even if set on the keyboard, have to be inserted in the type-matter by hand. A skilled craftsman's time is costly. The fewer corrections the better for all concerned with the production. If proofs are in page form, costs are multiplied enormously, as it is possible the formes have already been made up and locked in position to give you the perfect proofs. If it is absolutely essential at this later stage to correct, always ensure that any space caused by deletions will be filled by substituted letters or words, or, if a word or words are to be completely omitted an insertion of new matter is made to fill the space. The most expensive form of correction is that which involves the overrunning of matter from page to page in an imposed proof.

centre/
×/
∿/
less# (
⌒ ⌒/
eq.#/

[FINE ARTS, LITERATURE, *and* SCIENCE]
    / s.c.
    =

in England also, that for the past fifty years discovery had followed
upon discovery. And with rare exceptions the English Government adopted towards Science an attitude of absolute and impenetrable apathy. It is in Nonconformist England/the England
excluded from the national universities, in industrial England with
its new centres of population and civilization, that we must seek
the institutions which gave birth to the scientific and utilitarian
culture of the new era. That culture spread and made its way into
the old England of the aristocracy, and even into the universities.
But its birth was elsewhere. The thesis of historical materialism,
questionable when applied universally, is to this extent true of
England at the opening of the nineteenth century. Scientific
theory was the offspring of industrial practice. The emotional
piety of Evangelical religion and the hunger for experimental
knowledge developed at the same time, with the same intensity,
and in the same social *milieu.*

∠,
/ trs.
) T
=
∠ #
/ |
/ Stet
/ Bold
/ ℓ

XIV

Books were the medium in which the education of the middle
class was generated, in a sense, spontaneously. For half a century
past the literature of science had been daily enriched by new publications—some more technical, others more popular—adapted
thus to all the needs of different classes of readers.

The *Encyclopædia Britannica*, planned on the model of the *Encyclopédie* of Diderot and D'Alembert, had passed through five
editions since 1771/The first had been in three volumes—the fifth,
a quite recent publication, consisted of twenty. And the Publisher,
Constable, was arranging for an enormous supplement to be
written by the most eminent authorities of the day—a collection
of scholarly articles designed to present a complete picture of the
state of human knowledge about the year 1815. The venerable
Cyclopædia of Chambers, which had once served as the model of
the French *Encyclopédie*, had also passed through several editions.
Abraham Rees, after revising it for the first time in 17/, had
just undertaken at Longmans's invitation a new edition, which
would begin to appear in 1819 and would comprise thirty/nine
volumes. In addition to these works of general information numerous periodicals issued yearly and even monthly kept the public in
touch with the progress of science. Nicholson's Journal had just begun

⌒/
n.p. /
⊙
≡/
w.f./
↰/
×/
⸗ n.p./
take over

/Ital.
/⤸
/(P) l.c.
∠ 78
/-/
/ ⊐/Ital.
≡

559

Specimen page to show proof corrections

NB   In current printing it is unlikely that any good printer would
allow page proofs to reach this stage: most of the corrections
would have been made on the galley-proofs, for correction of
page-proofs is very costly. It will be noted that not only
straightforward errors, but such points as centring, broken type,
spaces, etc., are all indicated. It is a safe rule to query any
faint or blotchy impression, even though the fault may be due
to hurry: this will ensure that the printer overlooks no important point.

FINE ARTS, LITERATURE, AND SCIENCE

in England also, that for the past fifty years discovery had followed upon discovery. And with rare exceptions the English Government adopted towards Science an attitude of absolute and impenetrable apathy. It is in Nonconformist England, the England excluded from the national universities, in industrial England with its new centres of population and civilization, that we must seek the institutions which gave birth to the utilitarian and scientific culture of the new era. That culture spread and made its way into the old England of the aristocracy, and even into the universities. But its birth was elsewhere. The thesis of historical materialism, questionable when applied universally, is to this extent true of England at the opening of the nineteenth century. Scientific theory was the offspring of industrial practice. The emotional piety of Evangelical religion and the hunger for experimental knowledge developed at the same time, with the same intensity, and in the same social *milieu*.

XIV

Books were the medium in which the education of the middle class was generated, in a sense, spontaneously. For half a century past the literature of science had been daily enriched by new publications—some more technical, others more popular—adapted thus to the needs of different classes of readers.

The *Encyclopædia Britannica*, planned on the model of the *Encyclopédie* of Diderot and D'Alembert, had passed through five editions since 1771. The first had been in three volumes—the fifth, a quite recent publication, consisted of twenty. And the publisher, Constable, was arranging for an enormous supplement to be written by the most eminent authorities of the day—a collection of scholarly articles designed to present a complete picture of the state of human knowledge about the year 1815. The venerable *Cyclopædia* of Chambers, which had once served as the model of the French *Encyclopédie*, had also passed through several editions. Abraham Rees, after revising it for the first time in 1778, had just undertaken at Longmans's invitation a new edition, which would begin to appear in 1819 and would comprise thirty-nine volumes.

In addition to these works of general information numerous periodicals issued yearly and even monthly kept the public in

559

Specimen page after correction by printer

NB This demonstrates the need for indicating every fault: the left-hand margin is still out of alignment, the V of XIV is now broken off at the base, the comma after intensity is now indistinguishable from a period, and the 9 of 1819 badly printed.

Specimen of corrected page of index

158

National Council of Social Service's *Compilation of County Bibliographies,* 113

National Film Library, 102

New York State Library Indexing, 121

Newspapers, 42
    indexes, 14, 115
    reference sources, 103–4

Objects of art, 84–5

Office indexing, 81–2, 122

Open Letter to a Publisher, An, 72, 114

Organisations, 33–5

Oriental names, 140

Osborn's *Literature and Life,* 9, 122

Oxford Companion to English Literature, 143

Oxford Dictionary of Quotations, 143

Oxford English Dictionary, 141

Page proofs, 23–4

Page references, 23, 68–70

Paintings, 84–5

Palmer's *Index,* 14, 115

Paragraph headings, 11

Paragraph references, 23, 65, 138

Parish registers, 85–6

'Perfect Index, The', 30

Performers (music), 93–6

Periodicals
    abbreviation of titles, 107
    identification, 42–3, 49
    indexing, 103–9
    published indexes, 15, 108–9, 116
    reference sources, 49, 103–4, 107
    society publications, 49–50

Personal names, 31–3
    arrangement, 139
    rules, 137, 139, 140

Photographs, 82–3

Phrase and Fable, Dictionary of, 143

Pictures, 84–5

Place-names, 35–6, 41

Place subdivisions, 132–4

Plural headings, 52

Pollard's *Arrangement of Bibliographies,* 113

Poole's *Index,* 14

Pope, 139

Popular headings, 27–8, 136

Post Office telephone directories, 67–8, 116

Prefixes, 38–9, 140

Preparation for print, 60–74

Preparation of Manuscripts and Correction of Proofs, 124

Printer's style, 36

Printing, 60–74
    space estimates, 24–5, 72, 135

Private correspondence, 79–81

Proof correction, 71, 74
    examples, 126–9
    guides, 123, 124

Proofreading and Copy-preparation, 123

Public Affairs Information Service Bulletin, 116

Punch, 14

Punctuation, 61–2

Quotations, 143

Readers' Guide to Periodical Literature, 15, 116
    entry arrangement, 108–9

Reader's viewpoint, 38, 40

Reading lists, 110

Records, Gramophone, *see* Gramophone records

Records, Local, 85–6

The printers have made the corrections indicated on opposite page but, in
doing so, have introduced six new errors. Can you discover them?

Subdivisions
for places

An index without the articulating and clarifying device of cross-reference seldom does justice to the material.

E. M. HATT

THE SUBDIVISION OF NUMEROUS ENTRIES under the names of countries, large cities, etc., is by no means easy, and it is well to have a standard list of subdivisions which can be adapted and applied at will. Below is given a table of the subdivisions used by four famous reference works under the heading GREAT BRITAIN, from which the reader can choose or construct a list to suit his own requirements. In the case of the encyclopaedias only the main subdivisions are given, many of the items included in the main sequence of the two year books being grouped in the encyclopaedias in paragraph form under the main headings. The entries from the year books are not complete: they are a selection of the more usual entries likely to be needed for index work.

It will be noticed that the first three examples are arranged in alphabetical order, while *Chambers's Encyclopaedia* prefers to group its entries under main headings arranged according to a classification scheme of its own. The entries are, however, so clearly set out, that the lack of alphabetical arrangement seems no great disadvantage.

It is instructive to study the minor variations in the form of heading chosen by these different authorities: the *Statesman's Year-Book* uses the word 'Industries', *Chambers's* prefers 'Industry and Manufacture'; the *Britannica* uses 'Communication and Transportation', but the *Statesman's Year-Book* and *Chambers's* prefer 'Communications'. *Whitaker's* selects the heading 'Party Government', the *Statesman's Year-Book* 'Political Parties'.

Note, too, the *Britannica's* reference to 'English History' as a separate heading, a wise decision, for it gives a different position to a group of entries which, if placed within the heading GREAT BRITAIN, would occupy so much space as to conceal the arrangement of nearby entries.

Whitaker's Almanack	Encyclopaedia Britannica	Statesman's Year-Book	Chambers's Encyclopaedia
Agriculture	Agriculture	Agriculture	Agriculture
Air Transport	Colonies	Air Force	Industry and
Area and	Commerce and	Area and	Manufacture
Population	Industries	Population	Trade
Army	Communication	Census	Finance and
Banks and	and Transpor-	Churches	Banking
Banking	tation	Cities and	Communications
British Constitu-	Constitution and	Boroughs	Government and
tion	Government	Commerce	Judiciary
Census	Defence:	Communications	Armed Forces
Central Govern-	Air Force	Constitution and	and Defence
ment	Army	Government	Population and
Climate	Navy	Criminal	Health
Crime	Economics	Statistics	Social Condi-
Education	Education	Defence	tions
Employment	Finance	Education	Education
Exports	Fisheries	Exports	Religion
Fisheries	History, see	Finance	Archaeology
Government	English His-	Fisheries	Art
Imports	tory	Government	
Judicature	Labour	Imperial and	
Legislature	Law and Justice	Central	
Literature	Learned	Imports	
Local Govern-	Societies	Industries	
ment	Minerals	Labour and	
Maps	Population	Employment	
Merchant Navy	Social Questions	Local Govern-	
Meteorology		ment	
Minerals		Mining and Metals	
National		National	
Insurance		Insurance	
Occupations		Navy	
Parliament		Parliament	
Party Government		Police Force	
Population		Political Parties	
Production		Power, Water,	
Railways		Gas and Electri-	
Rainfall		city	
Religion		Production and	
Roads		Industry	
Royal Air Force		Railways	

N

Whitaker's Almanack	*Encyclopaedia Britannica*	*Statesman's Year-Book*	*Chambers's Encyclopaedia*
Royal Navy		Religion	
Scotland		Revenue and	
Shipping		Expenditure	
Taxation		Shipping	
Trade		Taxation	
Unemployment		Transport, Road	
Vital Statistics		Universities	
Wales		Weights and	
Wars		Measures	
Weather			

Table of number of index entries per page

Below is given a table of the number of possible index entries on each size of page in each of three sizes of type. In calculating the total number of possible entries, multiply by the number of pages allocated to the index, and subtract sufficient to allow for any indentation of the title and explanation of the Index on the first page, and for any later insertions—say, a minimum of thirty entries. The figures given below allow for the spaces necessary between each letter of the alphabet.

Size of Page	8 Pt. Single Column	8 Pt. Double Column	10 Pt. Single Column	10 Pt. Double Column	12 Pt. Single Column	12 Pt. Double Column
Foolscap 16mo	28	55	22	43	18	35
Crown	33	65	26	51	22	43
Demy	37	73	29	57	24	47
Medium	39	77	30	59	25	49
Royal	42	83	33	65	28	55
Foolscap 8vo	46	91	36	71	30	59
Crown	50	99	39	77	33	65
Demy	60	119	47	93	40	79
Medium	62	123	48	95	41	81
Royal	69	137	55	109	46	91
Foolscap 4to	57	113	45	89	37	73
Crown	67	133	53	105	44	87
Demy	76	151	60	119	50	99
Medium	78	155	61	121	51	101
Royal	85	169	68	135	56	111
Foolscap Folio	92	183	72	143	61	121
Crown	103	205	82	163	68	135
Demy	121	241	97	193	80	159
Medium	125	249	99	197	83	165
Royal	139	277	111	221	92	183

Twenty basic rules for indexers

1. Index everything useful in the book—text, illustrations, appendices, foreword, notes, bibliographies, etc.

2. Include all index entries in one alphabetical sequence.

3. Choose popular headings, with references from their scientific equivalents, except where a specialist audience is addressed.

4. Be consistent in choosing one form of spelling—seismography or seismology; ae or e, etc. Use a standard dictionary such as the *Concise Oxford* as your authority.

5. Choose the most specific headings which describe the items indexed: Steam-Boilers, not Boilers; Finance—Haiti, not Finance or Haiti alone, etc. Use phrases as headings if generally accepted: Training within industry; Social life and customs; but not Disposal of surplus stores; Rights of the human person, etc.

6. Be consistent in the use of singular or plural terms.

7. Combine the word and the action which describes it, where it is useful and possible: Banks and Banking; but not Fish and Fishing, etc.

8. Invert headings, where necessary, to bring significant word to the fore: Agriculture, Co-operative; Sociology, Christian, etc.

9. Check for synonyms and make suitable references from forms not used: Clothes, with references from Dress, and from Costume, etc.

196

10. Check for antonyms and combine where suitable; Employment and Unemployment, etc.

11. Where words of the same spelling represent different meanings, include identifying phrase in brackets: Race (sport); Race (ethnology), etc.

12. Where possible, give full names of persons quoted: Darwin, Erasmus; not Darwin, etc.

13. Omit the name of the country of a government department, in favour of direct entry under the subject: Trade, Board of; not Great Britain—Board of Trade, etc.

14. Use capitals for all proper names, and where the usage of foreign languages demands them: Aristotle; Menelaus; but, silage; quantum theory. Ruhe; Zweifel; but paix; guerre, etc.

15. Make references from main subjects to subdivisions of these subjects, and to related subjects: Costume, see also Gloves; Shoes; Hats, etc. But avoid a 'vicious circle' of references leading the reader back to the first heading.

16. Subdivide alphabetically by aspects wherever possible, to avoid long lists of page numbers.

17. In the case of historical and biographical works, substitute chronological for alphabetical subdivision, where this will definitely assist the reader.

18. Spell out symbols and abbreviations, except where the meaning of the abbreviations is not generally known. United Nations, not U.N.; but UNESCO, not United Nations Educational, Scientific and Cultural Organisation, etc.

19. Avoid the use of bold type wherever possible: use instead italics, capitals, parentheses, and any other legitimate typographical devices for distinguishing items.

20. If references are made to paragraph numbers and not to page numbers, include a note to this effect at the foot of every page of the index.

A dozen
rules for
arranging
index entries

The inclusion of an index is, of course, not enough in itself. It must be a good index.
THE TIMES, 8 May 1957

1. Arrange all entries in strict alphabetical order, even where a slight breaking of the sequence would allow nearly-related headings to come together.

2. Arrange entry headings word by word, ignoring any words after the comma in the case of inverted headings:

   > Fort de France
   > Fort Jameson
   > Fort Worth
   > Forth, The
   > Fortune Island

3. Ignore definite and indefinite articles in arrangement. Omit them where possible; where it is necessary to retain them, invert:

   > *Times, The*   *Temps, Le*

4. Where words of the same spelling represent different things, arrange in the following order:

(1) Persons	(3) Subjects
(2) Places	(4) Titles

5. Names used sometimes as Christian names, and sometimes as surnames, should be arranged in the following order:

(1) Saints	(3) Emperors and Kings
(2) Popes	(4) Surnames

6. Arrange double-barrelled names under first part of name, with reference from second part.

7. Treat M', Mc, Mac as though all were spelt Mac, for purposes of arrangement.

8. Treat hyphenated words as two separate words.

9. In the case of St., Ste., arrange as though spelt in full:

    Saint, Sainte

10. Ignore apostrophes and treat as though one word:

    O'Dowd; Shepheard's; etc.

11. Ignore prefixes such as *Lord*; *Mrs.*; *Viscount*; etc., for purposes of arrangement:

    Lang, *Mrs.* Alfred
    Lang, *Baron* Edwin

12. Include name prefixes in English and American names:

    De la Mare, Walter   Dos Passos, John

    In French names, include prefixes consisting of or containing the definite article. Invert others:

    La Fontaine, Jean de   *but*   Balzac, Honoré de
    Des Moines, Albert

    In other languages invert the prefix:

    Cervantes Saavedra, Miguel de
    Richthofen, Hugo von

    In the case of oriental names, use the form most likely to be remembered, and refer from other forms:

    Tagore, Rabindranath   with reference from
                            Rabindranath Tagore
    Yee, Chiang   with reference from
                            Chiang Yee

    When in doubt, consult the usage of a good standard biographical dictionary or, in the case of current personalities, *The Times Index*, or the name indexes of *Keesing's Contemporary Archives*.

The indexer's reference library

EVERY MAN NEEDS a few reference works to which he can turn in his own home. In the case of the indexer, a handful of well-chosen books may save him many mistakes and some journeys. Below is listed a selection of basic reference works on which the indexer can rely for the solution of his more usual difficulties, and where these fail him a telephone call to his nearest public library will almost invariably secure him the correct answer immediately.

ENCYCLOPAEDIA For those who have not room for the larger encyclopaedias, the one-volume *Columbia Encyclopedia* (Columbia University Press, 1963) will prove a compact and reliable standby at a reasonable price.

DICTIONARY *The Shorter Oxford English Dictionary on Historical Principles*, 3rd ed. rev. 2 volumes (Oxford, Clarendon Press, 1964) is the best medium-size dictionary on the market. For those with little book space, the *Concise Oxford Dictionary*, 5th edition (Oxford, Clarendon Press, 1964), will meet all ordinary requirements.

ALMANAC *Whitaker's Almanack* (Whitaker), published annually, is 'the most comprehensive single volume of general reference'. Its American counterpart, *World Almanac* (New York, World-Telegram), also published annually, is well worth buying too, for it is equally international in scope.

BIOGRAPHY For famous people of the past *Chambers's Biographical Dictionary*, new edition (Chambers, 1968), or *Webster's Biographical Dictionary* (Bell, 1970), or Albert M. Hyamson's *A Dictionary of Universal Biography of All Ages and All People*, 2nd edition (Routledge, 1951), will provide the essential dates and facts. Hyamson gives only one-line entries, but provides references to entries in the standard reference works. For living people *Who's Who* (Black), published annually, gives more than three thousand pages packed with information concerning not only British, but also Commonwealth and foreign persons of note. There are also five cumulative volumes of *Who Was Who*, covering the years 1897 to 1960.

NATIONS AND COUNTRIES

The Statesman's Year-Book (Macmillan), published annually, is an indispensable guide to the countries of the world, giving details and statistics of their government, finance, population, trade, education, religion, etc. As in the case of *Who's Who*, *Whitaker's Almanack*, and the *World Almanac*, old copies of the *Statesman's Year-Book* are well worth keeping as long as there is shelf space, for the sake of the statistics and political information they contain.

ATLAS AND GAZETTEER

The National Geographic (1966) *Atlas of the World* contains political maps of individual countries, physical and political maps of continents, and many different kinds of specialised information. A cheaper but very useful work is the *Advanced Atlas* (Bartholomew), of which a new edition was published in 1962. In addition to the indexes to these atlases, it is well to have a good gazetteer, such as *Webster's Geographical Dictionary* (Bell, 1966), a new quick-reference source of information covering more than forty-thousand places, and including 177 maps. For those dealing with historical material William R. Shepherd's *Historical Atlas*, 9th edition (University of London Press, 1964), is an excellent work for identifying the old names of places and discovering their modern equivalents.

DICTIONARY OF DATES

The outstanding events of the world are chronologically arranged and adequately indexed in William L. Langer's *Encyclopaedia of World History, Ancient, Medieval and Modern*, revised edition (Harrap, 1969). Another useful work is S. H. Steinberg's *Historical Tables, 58 BC–AD 1965*, 8th edition (Macmillan, 1966), which gives the outstanding events in classified tabular form.

SYNONYMS AND ANTONYMS

The best source for synonyms and antonyms is Peter Mark Roget's *Thesaurus of English Words and Phrases*, revised edition (Longmans, Green, 1941, reprinted frequently). There is also Roget's *International The-saurus*, 3rd edition (New York, Crowell, 1962).

ALLUSIONS

Allusions are often made by authors to various events and personalities both modern and classical which may not be so familiar to their readers. An excellent source for identifying many of these is the Rev. E. Cobham Brewer's *A Dictionary of Phrase and Fable*, 9th edition (Cassell, 1970), and another helpful volume is Sir Paul Harvey's *The Oxford Companion to English Literature*, 4th edition (Oxford, Clarendon Press, 1967). For unidentified quotations *The Oxford Dictionary of Quotations*, 3rd revised edition (Oxford, Clarendon Press, 1956), gives the more memorable words of both British and foreign writers and speakers.

SUBJECT-
HEADINGS

The best reference work on the choice of subject-headings is the Library of Congress Subject Cataloguing Division's *Subject Headings Used in the Dictionary Catalogue of the Library of Congress*, 6th edition (Washington, 1957), a monumental work of over twelve hundred pages. For home use, an Australian work: Heather Sherrie and Phyllis Mander Jones's *Short List of Subject Headings* (Angus & Robertson, 1950), will be found very helpful, while Bertha Margaret Frick's revision of *Sear's List of Subject Headings*, 9th edition (New York, H. W. Wilson, 1965), is a more detailed but still handy work. Unfortunately no British list of subject-headings has so far been published, and allowance will be necessary in using any of these works for some differences in the use of some words.

FILING

For the more abstruse problems of large-scale arrangement and filing of index slips, the *A.L.A. Rules for Filing Catalogue Cards* (revised edition. Chicago, American Library Association, 1968) and the British Standards Institution's *Alphabetical arrangement* (BS 1749: 1968) provide most of the answers in clear and logical form.

REFERENCE
BOOKS

It is often useful to know something of the main contents of other reference works in order to save time when searching for information. Constance M.

Winchell's *Guide to reference books*, 8th edition (Chicago, American Library Association, 1967), and A. J. Walford's *Guide to reference material*, 2nd edition (London, The Library Association, 1966–71), between them ensure that no reliable source of information—apart from specialist lines of research—is overlooked. Careful study of these two great works can save hours of misguided searching. Supplements to both Winchell and Walford are issued from time to time.

An
examination
for indexers

Index-making has been supposed to be 'a task that requires neither the light of learning nor the activity of genius, but may be successfully performed without any higher quality than that of bearing burthens with dull patience, and beating the track of the alphabet with sluggish resolution.'

SAMUEL JOHNSON (1709–84)

IN GREAT BRITAIN there are unfortunately no regular courses of training or qualifying examinations for indexers, whereas in the United States of America university courses—such as that conducted by Mr. John Askling at Columbia University—have been running for some time now. The situation may change in Great Britain since the Society of Indexers, which was formed in 1957, has the problem well in mind. In the meantime, indexers may like to try their hand at the following specimen examination paper which sets out to test their perception and ingenuity in this most exacting art. *When you have finished*, turn to page 205 for outline answers. No time limit is strictly necessary, but the whole paper could easily be done in two hours.

A. *Theoretical*

1. If you have 520 entries to print in four pages, indicate what size of type and what setting you would recommend so that all the entries can be accommodated.

2. Glance at the index at the end of this book and, without consciously counting, estimate the total number of entries in it.

3. An author on being urged by his publisher to make himself responsible for the index as well as the text of his book, and that he must therefore allow some time for indexing after the book has been completed, replies airily that his

grasp of the subject is sufficient to allow him to index as he goes. What is wrong with this statement?

4. A printer wrote to a publisher and said that if the proposal to add a single page to the index in a 320-page book were adopted, it would be necessary to increase the size of the volume to 336 pages. Why was this so? And what modifications would you suggest so that the index could be fully printed without increasing the size of the book?

5. An indexer finds to his chagrin on opening a new book for whose index he is responsible, that all the index entries after page 240 are one page out—i.e. a reference to page 259 is printed 258, one to 273 is given as 272, and so on. Outline the possible causes which could have occasioned this mishap.

6. You are asked to index the latest volume of a well-known illustrated periodical. Outline for the Editor the kinds of entries you would recommend for inclusion, and also any types of material which you feel might safely be omitted.

B. *Practical*

1. Make suitable marginal and text marks against the following index entries so that the first word is printed in small capitals; the second entry in italics; the fifth, sixth and seventh are indented under the fourth, and the two words of the last entry are transposed.

> Bewick, Thomas, 156
> Bible Pictures for Children, 123
> Blocks, drawing, 20
> Board, Bristol, 151, 169
> drawing, 21, 86
> straw, 21, 182
> water colour, 155
> Book illustration, 177
> Book jackets, 178
> Board, Bristol, 151, 169

2. Arrange the following index entries in alphabetical order (*a*) letter by letter, (*b*) word by word:

> Christian IX (Denmark)
> Christ Church, Oxford

Christ's Hospital
Christmas Island
Christian Chronology
Christchurch (N.Z.)
Christianity
Christ's College, Cambridge
Christmas Day

3. Give the correct index entries and any necessary references for the following proper names:

Simon de Montfort
William Rufus
Edward Sackville-West
Daphne du Maurier
Siam
Ghana
Tanzania
Trinidad and Tobago

Appendixes

Constitution and rules of the Society of Indexers

THE SOCIETY OF INDEXERS, believed to be the only association of its kind, was founded in London in 1957. Its Constitution, as revised in 1969, is given here in full, for it reflects the aims of all serious indexers.

1 NAME

The name of the Society shall be THE SOCIETY OF INDEXERS (hereinafter called the Society).

2 OBJECTS

The objects of the Society are:

Standard of indexing — (*a*) to improve the standard of indexing and to secure some measure of uniformity in technique;

Register of Indexers — (*b*) to maintain registers of indexers in all fields from which authors, editors, publishers and others may be furnished with suitable names on application;

Advisory body — (*c*) to act as an advisory body on the qualifications and remuneration of indexers to which authors, editors, publishers and others may apply for guidance;

Publications — (*d*) to publish or communicate from time to time books, papers and notes on the subject of indexing;

Status and interests — (*e*) to raise the status of indexers and to safeguard their interests.

3 MEMBERSHIP

Classes of membership — (*a*) Membership of the Society shall be open to *bona fide* indexers, librarians, cataloguers, archivists, information-filing experts and such other persons interested in promoting the objects of the Society as the Council may approve. Corporate and other bodies, firms and associations shall be eligible for institutional membership at the discretion of the Council. (The word 'member' shall, unless otherwise stated, include 'institutional member'.) Honorary life membership may be awarded at a General Meeting to a member of the Society or other person who has rendered meritorious service to indexing or the Society, the total number of honorary life members not to exceed five at any given time.

Representatives of Institutional members (b) Representatives of institutional members shall enjoy all the privileges of membership except that they shall not be eligible for election to office or to the Council.

Applications (c) Application for membership shall be made on the appropriate forms and addressed to the General Secretary who shall refer such application (other than in the case of Founder Members) to the Council. The decision of the Council as to eligibility for membership shall be final.

Removal from membership (d) The Council shall have power to remove from the list of members the name of any member who, in the opinion of the Council, acts in any way detrimental to the interests of the Society. Any former member whose name has been so removed shall have a right of appeal against the removal at the next Annual General Meeting, provided notice of intention to appeal shall have been given in writing to the General Secretary within threeweeks of the Council's decision being communicated to the former member.

4 REGISTER OF INDEXERS

Register of Indexers (a) The Council shall maintain a classified register of indexers. In approving the admission of members to the register the Council shall take into consideration a member's standing as an indexer, the number of indexes for which he has been responsible and the quality of his work. The decision of the Council as to eligibility for admission to the register shall be final. The inclusion of a member's name in the register shall entitle that member to be known as a Registered Indexer of the Society of Indexers so long as he or she remains a member of the Society.

(b) No fee shall be payable for admission to the register or for the furnishing of names therefrom to authors, editors, publishers or other persons.

5 SUBSCRIPTIONS AND FINANCE

Subscriptions (a) Each member shall pay such annual subscriptions as may from time to time be determined at an Annual

General Meeting. Subscriptions shall be payable in advance and shall fall due on the 1st April in every year. Members joining after the 31st December in any year shall pay half of the annual subscription for the remainder of that financial year.

Withdrawal (*b*) Members shall be liable for their annual subscriptions until notice in writing to withdraw from membership shall have been received by the General Secretary.

Arrears (*c*) Members whose subscription is twelve months in arrears shall automatically cease to be members of the Society. Such former members wishing to re-join the Society may do so on payment of arrears or such lesser sum as the Council may determine.

Life (*d*) The annual subscription of individual members membership may be commuted by the payment of a single subscription equivalent to ten times the amount of the annual subscription applicable at the time of such commutation; such payments shall be assigned to the capital assets of the Society. Members who have so commuted shall be designated Life Members. For honorary life membership see clause 3(*a*).

Bank (*e*) A bank account shall be opened in the name of account the Society. Cheques shall be signed by the Treasurer or, in his absence, the Chairman or Vice-Chairman, and countersigned by the General Secretary or, in his absence, the Assistant General Secretary.

6 PRESIDENT AND VICE-PRESIDENTS

A distinguished person may be elected President of the Society at the Annual General Meeting. Vice-Presidents up to a total of six may be elected, particularly in respect of members who have rendered notable service to the Society, such elections to be made at a General Meeting.

7 OFFICERS AND COUNCIL

Officers (*a*) The Officers of the Society shall consist of a Chairman, Vice-Chairman, Treasurer, General Secretary and an Assistant General Secretary, and Membership Secretary who shall be elected at the Annual General Meeting. The Officers shall be eligible for re-election in consecutive years.

Council (*b*) The Council shall consist of the Officers and six
members to be elected at the Annual General Meeting, the President and Vice-Presidents being *ex officio*
members. The six members shall retire in rotation,
two at each Annual General Meeting but shall be
eligible for re-election. The two members to retire in
every year shall be those who have been longest in
office since the last election, but as between persons
who became members on the same day those to retire
shall be determined by lot.

Elections (*c*) Nominations for office or membership of the
Council shall be signed by two members of the
Society and countersigned by the nominee. They
must reach the General Secretary not later than one
calendar month before the date of the Annual
General Meeting. A list of candidates for election
shall be circulated by the General Secretary to the
members not later than 21 days before the meeting.
Voting shall be by show of hands, but members unable to attend may record their votes by letter to
reach the General Secretary not later than the first
post on the day preceding the Annual General Meeting. Postal votes shall be counted by the Honorary
Auditors or, in the absence of one or both of them, by
a member or members appointed for the purpose at
the meeting.

Council (*d*) Casual vacancies on the Council or in any of the
vacancies offices shall be filled by invitation of the Council, and
the persons filling such vacancies shall hold office
only until the next following Annual General Meeting and shall then be eligible for re-election, but
shall not be taken into account in determining the
members who are to retire by rotation at that
meeting.

Co-opted (*e*) The Council shall be empowered to co-opt an-
members nually one representative each from the Library
Association and ASLIB. Co-opted members shall not
have the right to vote in Council on any matter
affecting the conduct of the Society or the status of
its members unless themselves members of the
Society. The Council shall also be empowered to
invite organizations to send observers to meetings of
the Council.

Council *(f)* The Council shall meet not less often than once
meetings every three months. The Secretary may, with the
approval of the Chairman or, in his absence, the
Vice-Chairman, summon a special meeting of the
Council at other times. Five members of the Council
shall form a quorum.

Annual *(g)* The Council shall prepare an Annual Report
Report and Statement of Income and Expenditure for sub-
mission to the Annual General Meeting.

8 MEETINGS

Society *(a)* The Annual General Meeting shall be held not
meetings later than the last day of May in each year at some
place to be decided by the Council. Not less than
twenty-one days' notice of the Annual General Meeting shall be given to all members of the Society by
the General Secretary.

A.G.M. *(b)* The business of the Annual General Meeting
shall include:

    (i) the election of Officers and the requisite
number of Council members as provided for
in clause 7*(b)* above;

    (ii) the consideration of the Annual Report sub-
mitted by the Council;

    (iii) the consideration of an audited Statement
of Income and Expenditure for the past year;

    (iv) the election of two Auditors not being mem-
bers of the Council.

Special *(c)* On the receipt by the Chairman or General
General Secretary of a written requisition signed by not fewer
Meetings than ten members, the Council shall call a Special
General Meeting to be held within twenty-one days
of the receipt of the requisition. Not less than fourteen
days' notice of a Special General Meeting shall be
given to all members by the General Secretary, unless
in the opinion of the Council the urgency of the
business to be transacted and resolutions to be proposed makes a shorter notice necessary. No other
business shall be entertained.

(d) The Council may at any time call a Special
General Meeting and such Special General Meeting
shall be subject to the same provision as to notice
and business set out in clause *(c)* above.

(e) The place and time of a Special General Meeting shall be decided by the Chairman or, in his absence, by the Vice-Chairman.

Quorum (f) A quorum of an Annual General or Special General Meeting shall be formed by ten members, personally present and each entitled to vote.

9 COMMITTEES

Special Committees (a) The Council shall be empowered to establish special Committees of the Society to represent bodies of members in special fields, including legal, medical, scientific, technical, and non-literary.

Chairmen and Secretaries (b) Special Committees shall appoint their own Chairmen and Secretaries and shall meet as and when the Chairman may decide. The Chairman and General Secretary of the Society shall be *ex officio* members of all Committees.

10 TRAINING AND FELLOWSHIPS

Training (a) The Council shall be empowered to organize teaching and training and to conduct examinations in the interests of the improvement of indexing.

Fellowships (b) The Council shall be empowered to award Fellowships to Members of the Society under such conditions as it may determine.

11 HONORARY CORRESPONDENTS

Correspondents The Council shall be empowered to appoint Honorary Correspondents overseas to represent the Society in countries and territories of the Commonwealth and in foreign countries so that the Society may be informed of developments in indexing and kindred matters in the countries in which the Correspondents reside.

12 DONATIONS AND LEGACIES

Donations, etc. The Society shall be authorized to accept donations and legacies for the furtherance of its aims and objects.

13 INTERVENTION

Disputes etc. (a) On the payment of a fee of one guinea members may request the Council to intervene in any dispute between them and any other person or body on any matter connected with indexing, and the Council may, if requested by the parties, act as arbitrator or appoint an arbitrator.

(*b*) In any case of intervention the member asking for the Council's assistance shall be responsible for all legal and other expenses incurred by the Council.

(*c*) The Council may refuse, without assigning reasons, to accede to a member's request for intervention, in which case the fee shall be refunded.

14 AMENDMENTS

Amendments to Constitution Amendments to the Constitution and Rules of the Society shall be made only at an Annual General Meeting or at a Special General Meeting called for the purpose. Proposals to amend the Constitution and Rules of the Society must be submitted to the Secretary not less than twenty-eight days before the date of the Annual General Meeting. In the case of proposals to be made at a Special General Meeting the rules as to notice contained in clause 8(*c*) above shall apply.

Outline
answers
to the
examination
paper

A. *Theoretical*

These are straightforward questions which demand little technical knowledge. The following points are suggested:

1. Assuming that the book is a Royal 8vo, double-column 8-point setting would give just sufficient space.

2. Approximately 750.

3. If the author is a superman, he could probably do this work satisfactorily. In any case, he can certainly make notes of the index entries, etc., he is likely to need. Whatever system he adopts, however, considerable editing will be needed on completion of the book to eliminate synonymous entries, ensure consistency, allow for after-thoughts, insert the page references (unless the book were being indexed by paragraph references), and review the whole index from the point of view of the reader.

4. From the printer's remarks it is evident that the book in question has sections of 16 pages each. To include an extra page of index, the following expedients (or a combination of some or all of them) are available: (*a*) small type, (*b*) double, or triple column setting, (*c*) grouping lengthy index entries in paragraph form, (*d*) cutting the size of the index by using more references, (*e*) eliminating space between alphabetical sections of the index.

5. This indicates that the present page 241 is a new page, inserted at the last moment. This can happen sometimes as a result of an emergency. Thus it might be decided to include an extra line block that could be printed with the text—the insertion, if the block were large, might result in every page reference onwards being wrong. Again, if 240 were the end of a chapter and it was decided to add a couple of paragraphs, this would

mean in many cases that the new chapter would now begin on page 242. The indexer's only remedy is to ask to be kept informed of every development up to the last moment.

6. (1) Personalities, (2) Places, (3) Events, (4) Signed articles. In such journals it might be safe to omit the 'features'—such as chess problems, book reviews, bridge notes, etc., none of which is likely to be outstanding in its field.

B. *Practical*

1. Bewick, Thomas, 156
   Bible Pictures for Children, 123
   Blocks, drawing, 20
   Board, Bristol, 151, 169
   [drawing, 21, 86

   [straw, 21, 182
   [water colour, 155
   Book illustration, 177
   Book jackets, 178
   Board, Bristol, 151, 169

2. *Letter by Letter*

   Christchurch (N.Z.)
   Christ Church, Oxford
   Christian Chronology
   Christian IX (Denmark)
   Christianity
   Christmas Day
   Christmas Island
   Christ's College, Cambridge
   Christ's Hospital

   Word by Word

   Christ Church, Oxford
   Christ's College, Cambridge
   Christ's Hospital
   Christchurch (N.Z.)
   Christian IX (Denmark)
   Christian Chronology
   Christianity
   Christmas Day
   Christmas Island

3. Montfort, Simon de, Earl of Leicester
   'see' references: De Montfort, Simon
   Leicester, Simon de Montfort, Earl of
   William II (William Rufus), King of England
   'see' references: William Rufus
   Rufus, William
   Sackville-West, Edward [Charles]
   'see' reference: West, Edward [Charles] Sackville-
   Du Maurier, Daphne [Lady Browning]
   'see' references: Maurier, Daphne du
   Browning, Lady

   Siam
   'see' reference: Thailand
   Ghana
   'see' references: Gold Coast
   Togoland

Tanzania
  'see' references: Tanganyika
                 Zanzibar

Trinidad and Tobago
  'see' reference: Tobago
  'see also' references: British Caribbean Federation
                       British West Indies
  'see' reference: West Indies, British

NB The additional names in the entries for Edward Sackville-West and Daphne Du Maurier would, in fact, only be included if there were relevent material in the text of the book, just as no-one ordinarily quotes Charles Dickens' full name. In the case of Tanzania, the 'see' references would become 'see also' references if there were material in the text relating to Tanganyika, etc., before they received their present designation.

Index

If the reader be not satisfied with this table, let him not blame the order, but his owne conceipt.

RAPHAEL HOLINSHED: The Chronicles of England, Scotland and Ireland, volume III (Index), 1587.

The reason why there is no Table or Index added hereunto is, that every page is so full of signal remarks that were they couch'd in an Index it wold make a volume as big as the book, and so make the Postern Gate to bear no proportion to the Building.

HOWELL: Discourse concerning the Precedency of Kings, 1664.

Printed in Great Britain
by The Bowering Press, Plymouth